T0299698

"This book delivers the authentic teaching of Shamanic Qigong and at the same time provides the cultural context that gave it birth. This sort of knowledge and understanding is rare nowadays, even among Chinese masters. How fortunate we are to have this volume from Master Wu Zhongxian, which he shares with us as the old friends we are on the oldest of paths."

– Red Pine (Bill Porter), author of The Road to Heaven

"Qigong integrates posture, movement, mind, and breath. Within Qigong there is softness and fluidity, strength and power, and internal focus and outward opening. Zhongxian Wu has performed a great service in deepening our knowledge of Qigong, offering both the form itself and his understanding of how to lead a harmonious Qigong life."

– Peter Deadman, author of A Manual of Acupuncture *and founder of* Journal of Chinese Medicine

"This energetic presentation of the worldview that informs the theory and practice of Shamanic Qigong is practical, easy to follow, and astonishingly comprehensive. Master Wu's lucid contemporary prose provides a valid passport to China's central province of healing: the appropriate regulation and deployment of the body. He talks to the reader as if to a friend across a table at a tea house, and he knows that if we each will only allow ourselves to accept the healing warmth he has poured out for us, the spirit of immediate living will fill our cup. We would be cranky to refuse."

– John Beebe, Jungian analyst, author of Integrity in Depth

"A seminal work in the field of Qigong. For Westerners interested in this fascinating healing art, it opens a window into the little-known Shamanic roots of Qigong. Master Wu's compassionate heart and sincere spirit offers readers a trusted guide through the cultural history of Chinese Shamanic Qigong and the practice of personal cultivation."

– Francesco Garri Garripoli, author of Qigong: Essence of the Healing Dance

Chinese Shamanic
Tiger Qigong

CHINESE SHAMANIC TIGER QIGONG

Embrace the Power of Emptiness

MASTER ZHONGXIAN WU

SINGING DRAGON

LONDON AND PHILADELPHIA

立席功

戊戌季夏 童圣

Chapter 5 is adapted from *Vital Breath of the Dao: Chinese Shamanic Tiger Qigong – Laohu Gong*. First published in the UK in 2008 by Singing Dragon, an imprint of Jessica Kingsley Publishers, and first published in the US in 2006 by Dragon Door Publications, Little Canada, MN 55164, USA, www.dragondoor.com

First published in 2019
by Singing Dragon,
an imprint of Jessica Kingsley Publishers
73 Collier Street
London N1 9BE, UK
and
400 Market Street, Suite 400
Philadelphia, PA 19106, USA

www.singingdragon.com

Library of Congress Cataloging in Publication Data
A CIP catalog record for this book is available from the Library of Congress

British Library Cataloguing in Publication Data
A CIP catalogue record for this book is available from the British Library

ISBN 978 1 84819 384 0
eISBN 978 0 85701 341 5

Printed and bound by CPI Group (UK) Ltd, Croydon CR0 4YY

For my darling daughter and
all future generations

Acknowledgements

In the time river and space ocean of our existence, I am profoundly grateful that this special, timeless drop of water, Chinese Shamanic Tiger Qigong, is still relevant and continues to nourish others.

I offer my deepest-heart-gratitude to all those who have kept our ancient wisdom alive.

I extend many, many thanks to Jessica Kingsley and to Singing Dragon for supporting my writing and for publishing my books.

Wordless appreciation flows to my family for their loving support of my practice, my teaching, and my writings, and especially to my wife, Karin Taylor Wu, who contributed her skillful editing and insight into this book.

HuZhou 虎咒 –
Tiger Incantation

Incantation Calligraphy by Master Zhongxian Wu

長庚之英白虎之精
陰陽相資山川效靈
憲天之則法地之寧
分列八卦順考五行
百靈無以逃其狀
卍物不能遁其形
得而寶之福祿來成

ChangGengZhiYing BaiHuZhiJing
YinYangXiangZi ShanChuanXiaoLing
XianTianZhiZe FaDiZhiNing
FenLieBaGua ShunKaoWuXing
BaiLingWuYiTaoQiZhuang WanWuBuNengDunQiXing
DeErBaoZhi FuLuLaiCheng

The spirit of Venus
The essence of White Tiger
The duo of YinYang
Emulating the soul of mountains and rivers
Reflecting the Heavenly Way
Ruling Earthly Peace
Exemplified as BaGua [Eight Trigrams]
Manifested as WuXing [Five Elements]
With it, hundreds of spirits cannot escape from their shapes
Ten-thousand-things is unable to hide from their forms
Obtain and treasure it
Blessings and prosperity are coming

The above incantation made its earliest appearance in the archeological record on a bronze mirror from the Sui 隋 Dynasty (581–619 CE), and it beautifully illustrates the boundless power of China's venerated tiger. This well-regarded invocation is one of my personal favorites for cultivation and healing work. I share it here with you in hope of awakening your inner Tiger and with wishes for great fortune to find you as you journey with Chinese Shamanic Tiger Qigong.

Contents

INTRODUCTION

It is 2018, twelve years since the publication of my first book in English, *Vital Breath of the Dao: Chinese Shamanic Tiger Qigong*. As I discussed in that book, twelve is a magic number!

> It is a symbol for the universal clock, i.e. ShiErChen 十 二 辰, representing time and space. In Chinese cosmology, we certainly recognize the number twelve as contained in the twelve Chen 辰 (1 Chen = 2 hours) in the day or the twelve months of the year. In Chinese medicine, the number twelve corresponds to the twelve organ meridian systems in the human body or microcosm, which in turn correspond to the twelve months in the year and the twelve spiritual animals related to the zodiac. Twelve represents the energetic changes our bodies experience in a twelve Chen day and the twelve months of the year as well.[1]

This book was widely acknowledged as a "modern Qigong classic" by readers all over the world and has been reprinted several times. Over the years, I have received countless requests from seasoned practitioners to expand upon my writings in *Vital Breath of the Dao*. As the number twelve also represents progression and new life, I find it is finally the perfect time for the original book to evolve – allow me to welcome you now to its new incarnation!

For this new enterprise, I have decided to elaborate upon my previous writing to the extent that it makes most sense to expand my first

---

1   Zhongxian Wu, *Vital Breath of the Dao: Chinese Shamanic Tiger Qigong*. St. Paul, MN: Dragon Door Publications, 2006, p.68.

book into two much larger stand-alone books. The *Chinese Shamanic Tiger Qigong* book you are currently reading is an extended version of the "Qigong practice" section of the original book. In the soon-to-be-published, extended edition of the main part of *Vital Breath of the Dao*, I have focused on adding considerably more detailed information on the shamanic roots of Qigong, Wu 巫 (Chinese shamanism) tradition, Daoism, symbolism, numerology, and philosophy.

The symbolic meanings of "Venerable Tiger" are deep and rich, and give shape to the very spirit of the Tiger Qigong form. Having taught this form to students all over the world since the early 1990s, I feel it is time to unlock some of the mystery of LaoHu 老虎 (Shamanic Tiger) by sharing a more advanced discussion on Tiger symbolism as it relates to this traditional internal cultivation practice. I have found that students are ever more ready to increase their understanding and heighten their experience of the Tiger Qigong practice, and that by delving further into Xiang 象 (Daoist symbolism) other practitioners seeking the essence of traditional Daoist internal arts also receive greater benefits from their own practice.

After years of specific requests from my senior students, I will also share how each movement in the Tiger Qigong practice relates to the eight extraordinary meridians, twelve organ meridians, and 24 JieQi. This previously secret knowledge will add dimension to your practice and help you develop your cultivation experience and optimize its healing results.

It is my hope that this new edition will support those of you on the path of holism, ancient healing techniques, and spiritual cultivation in gaining innumerable rewards from your own dedicated efforts.

Auspicious Qi,

Wu Zhongxian 吳忠賢

"Rainbow Harbor," Sweden

1

MEN 門

THE ENTRANCE

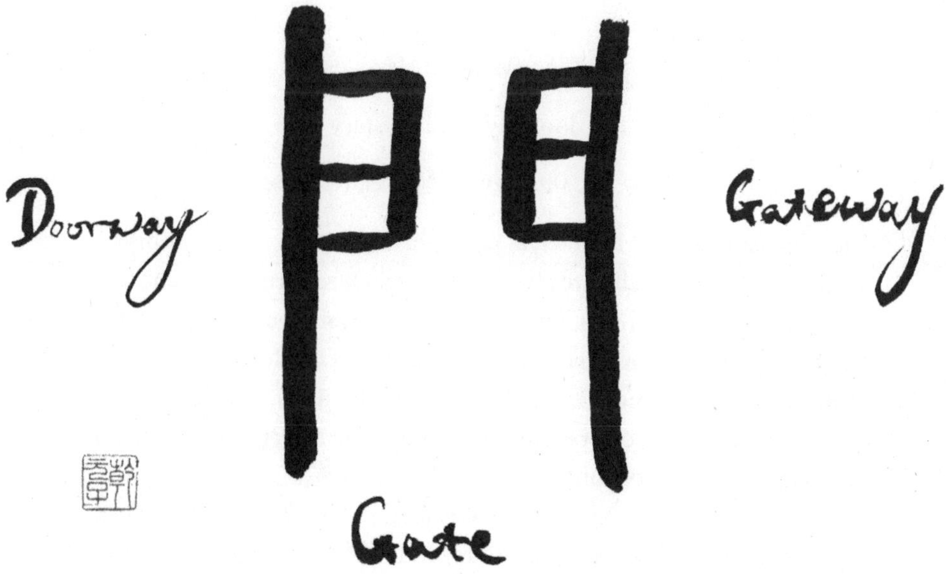

Doorway

門

Gateway

Gate

Men Calligraphy by Master Zhongxian Wu

眾
妙
之
門

ZhongMiaoZhiMen

The doorway of all mystery

– LaoZi 老子, *DaoDeJing* 道德經 (Chapter 1)

The Chinese character **Men** 門, at its origins, means gate, door, doorway, or gateway. Traditionally, we also use Men when referring to a school or lineage in art, martial arts, Qigong 氣功, religion, technology, and so forth. When you become a lineage disciple, for example, we refer to you as RuMen 入門 (someone who has entered the gate), which indicates that you will now have opportunities to learn the secret skills hidden in the "treasure house" of your master's art.

In order to effectively gain the essential cultivation methods from any classical Qigong lineage, please try to find the Men/Gate first, even if you are likely to never have a chance to learn directly from the lineage master. Here is a tip for doing so:

In my tradition (Wu 巫, or Chinese Shamanism), we understand that the name of an object also symbolizes all essence of said object. For instance, a new baby's name is not only used for communication purposes but it also contains the baby's personality and life karma. In Chinese, there is a saying, XingMingTianGongHao 姓名天公號 – "A person's name comes from the universe." In other words, it doesn't matter who gave you your name – the universe is the original inspiration of the name. The same holds true for the names of Qigong forms.

As LaoZi 老子 states in the first chapter of his *DaoDeJing* 道德經, YouMingWangWuZhiMu 有名萬物之母 ("A name is the mother of the ten-thousand-things"). The name of a Qigong form contains the essence and spirit of the form. Gaining a better understanding of the name is a secret entrance or doorway to connect with the spirit of the form in our practice. Therefore, let us start our Tiger Qigong journey together by learning the symbolic meanings of the form's name.

The original Chinese name for Tiger Qigong is LaoHu Gong 老虎功, which translates into English as Chinese Shamanic Tiger Qigong. The power of the form springs from its roots in the heart of Chinese Shamanism. It is a great tool for healing, for developing your martial arts skills, and for spiritual transformation. The Tiger form is also the story of energy circulation through the 24 seasons – the rhythm of the Dao itself. Learning the individual symbolic meanings of these three Chinese characters will not only help you tap into the essence of the form, but will also help you ground into the form's functions.

1.1 Lao 老
– To Be "Old"

Lao Calligraphy in Oracle Bone Script by Master Zhongxian Wu

Literally, **Lao** 老 means old. In Chinese, it is also a symbol for great wisdom. Of course, we all know that a person's wisdom isn't always directly correlated with his or her numerical age, but even today in modern China, "old" is used as a title to express respect. For instance, the Chinese word for "teacher" is LaoShi 老師 – which translates directly into English as "old master." In Chinese tradition, a teacher is one of the most respected jobs one can have. The function of a teacher used to be described as ChuanDaoShouYeJieHuo 傳道受業解惑 – "Pass the Dao, teach the techniques, and help students find the answers to their questions and doubts."[1] Regardless of age, teachers in China are still called "old master."

In ancient times, Wu 巫 (the Chinese shaman) held the most respected jobs (leader of a tribe, medicine man/woman, astronomer, agriculturist, philosopher, and so on) and teaching was an essential part of his or her role in society. The JiaGuWen 甲骨文, or ancient oracle bone style of writing, can help us better understand Lao 老. The written pattern of the oracle bone character for Lao resembles a person holding a staff.

In Chinese shamanism, a staff represents the power of the universe. Armed with a staff, a shaman had the power to pass on universal knowledge to others. Later, when teachers took over that aspect of the shaman's duty, they always taught with a small staff in their hands – a remnant of former times. The first time I looked at this oldest style of Chinese character, an image arose in my mind's eye: the Queen Mother of the West (XiWangMu 西王母) standing on the top of Kunlun Mountain, holding the victory staff in her hand – an image which still connects me to the original spirit of this form, every time I practice this Tiger Qigong form.

1.2 Hu 虎
– The Qi 气 Web Master

Hu Calligraphy in Oracle Bone Script by Master Zhongxian Wu

---

1   This citation is from the famous Tang 唐 Dynasty (617–907 CE) scholar Hanyu 韓愈's *Shishuo* 師說.

Hu 虎 means tiger. To Chinese, the tiger is an exceptionally powerful animal, protected by the strength of its skin, its weapons of "iron teeth and metal claws,"[2] its thunderous growl, and its ferociousness.

Stone tiger with cinnabar in its mouth, eyes, and ears, from JinSha 金沙 ancient ruin site in SiChuan 四川 province, China. In Chinese shamanic tradition, cinnabar has the function to release evil energy.

The tiger is known as the king of the beasts as the striped pattern on its forehead resembles the Chinese character Wang 王, or king. In ancient Chinese tradition, kings, generals, and judges were often depicted as officiating from chairs that were ceremoniously draped with a tiger skin. Warriors regularly used tiger skins on their shields, armor, and helmets to intimidate the enemy. Even today, Chinese living rooms often feature tiger images to keep intruders at bay and drive away any evil influences! Throughout history, the tiger has also held an important role in health and healing. For example, Chinese shamans were known to don tiger skins and masks for exorcism rituals, and a book on the subject of customs and mores from 195 CE describes the ability of the tiger to ShiShiGuiMei 噬食鬼魅 "devour demons and evil spirits."[3] Traditional medicine practitioners still use the tiger to drive out Yin 陰 (demons and diseases), a long-standing practice discussed in *BenCao GangMu* 本草綱目, the Ming Dynasty's herbal compendium – the most comprehensive volume of traditional Chinese medicine. For centuries, when met with bad fortune, Chinese people have believed that incinerating a tiger skin and drinking the ashes, or touching a tiger claw, will drive away malevolent forces.

---

2   Li Shizhen 李時珍 (1518–1593 CE), *Bencao Gangmu* 本草綱目.

3   YingShao 應劭 (153–196 CE), *Fengsu Tongyi* 風俗通義.

Often overlooked is the spiritual power embodied in the tiger. Chinese shamanism maintains that the striped pattern of tiger's skin represents the Dao itself, because the stripes looks like a repeating pattern of Qi 气 – the image of the web of the universe. As LaoZi states in Chapter 73 of the DaoDeJing, TianWangHuiHui ShuErBuShi 天網恢恢 疏而不失, which means the Heavenly Web (or the Qi Web) is vast, yet nothing escapes from its wide meshes. The tiger is the universal web master, weaving everything together.

Tiger web diagram by Master Zhongxian Wu

Through regular practice of the Chinese Shamanic Tiger Qigong form, you learn to access and channel the uncompromising power of the tiger. Harnessing this formidable inner resource allows you to be able to better respond to your "enemies," whether these enemies be externally or internally derived. Tiger Qigong, as well as other forms of traditional Qigong, can be both curative and restorative, teaching you how to work with disease and imbalance by using your own intrinsic healing abilities. In terms of personal cultivation techniques, the tiger is symbolic of many, many things: Lungs, breath, Qi 气, respiratory system, change, control, circulation, rule, rhythm, white, transparency, uprightness, justice, autumn, wind, and the seven Chinese lunar mansions in the Western sky.

As a totem of the great Dao, or the Master of the Qi Web, tiger holds even more symbolic meanings. In WuXing 五行, the Five Elements philosophy, tiger is the spiritual animal for the Western direction (of our universe), the Metal Element, Venus, and for the Lungs of the human body. Tiger is also a symbol of XiWangMu 西王母, the Queen Mother of the West. In Daoism, XiWangMu is of vital significance; not only is she considered to be the first and foremost ancestral master to pass Daoist teachings on to others, but she is also revered as the condensation of (the physical manifestation of) the Subtlest Vital Breath of the Western Essence from DaoQi 道炁 – in other words, the Vital Breath of the entire natural world, and that which keeps everything alive. The tiger, the Vital Breath of the Dao, also expresses itself as JieQi 節气, the 24 seasons of a year, and establishes the rhythm of our macrocosm.

Generally speaking, in Chinese shamanic tradition, tiger is known as BaiHu 白虎 – White Tiger. In Chinese culture, white does not merely mean the color white; rather, it is the symbol for transparency, clarity, purification, justice, punishment, and killing. "White" symbolizes the spiritual qualities of the tiger totem. In the natural world, we come to know about the spiritual White Tiger through observation of the "killing" atmosphere that directs the autumn season. This "killing" in autumn is the process that then generates new life to flourish in the spring season – it is the natural way to clear out old energy and weakness in order to build and maintain strong new life energy.

When autumn arrives, it brings with it strong winds to sweep down the leaves and break off the weak and sick branches from the trees. Come the following spring, these stripped trees often grow into stronger, healthier versions of their former selves. This natural "killing" function of the autumn season is mirrored in our spiritual bodies as a process controlled by the Lungs. In Chinese medicine, the function of the Lungs is to break up old energy (including dead and damaged cells), clear Qi stagnation, kill invading evil (e.g. microbes and pernicious influences), and maintain Qi circulation. In our bodies, the Lung is in charge of our ZhengQi 正气 (our Righteous/Upright/Centered Qi), which keeps pathogens from invading our bodies, and helps us maintain honorable thinking and make admirable lifestyle choices. We would all get very sick quickly without this protective "killing" function of Lung. In LaoHuGong, we deeply connect with the Tiger – the spiritual animal of the Lung, the very essence of Lung Qi, and the vital breath of the natural world. The 24 movements of the form correspond with the 24 JieQi of the annual cycle, which help bring you into resonance and harmony with the shifting energies of the 24 seasons. As a result, the just and mighty power of the Tiger strengthens your ZhengQi and your life, in all manner of ways.

Committed practitioners know the phrase: RenZaiQiZhong QiZaiRenZhong 人在气中 气在人中, which means that human beings are living within the Qi and Qi spreads within the human body. It is possible to experience this state of cultivation through a dedicated daily practice of Tiger Qigong. Similarly, the Tiger is within you and you are within the Tiger. I hope you use the Tiger to become a master of your own realm, weaving you ever more deeply into the harmonious and resilient web of the universe.

1.3 Gong 功
– Work Out

Gong Calligraphy in Oracle Bone Script by Master Zhongxian Wu

Originally, **Gong** 功 meant to work hard and in the correct way. It has come to mean, more generally speaking, work, feat, skill, merit, achievement, and it is also used to mean GongFu 功夫 (martial arts, anything worthy that takes a commitment of time, or simply time itself). When used in the title of a Qigong form, it is typically as an abbreviation of Qigong. To deepen our insight into this (or any traditional) form, let us take a closer look at the Chinese character for Gong.

This character contains the radical Gong 工 and the radical Li 力. Gong 工 means labor, project, skill, delicate, result, work, worker, and engineer. The original meaning of Gong 工 is the carpenter's square or ruler, which is a symbol of universal law. The second radical, Li 力 means all one's best, force, power, effort, and strength. The Han 漢 Dynasty (206 BCE–220 CE) dictionary *ShuoWen JieZi* 說文解字 explains Li as "a pattern of tendons." Therefore, Gong 功 hints at the meaning that a person should follow the correct way and work hard if he/she wants to improve his/her skill. With respect to Qigong, following the correct way not only means finding a traditional form, but also finding an upright and honorable teacher, and following his/her instruction precisely (please remember, a famous teacher is not always equivalent to an upright and honorable one…).

Through regular practice of the Tiger Qigong form, you will strengthen your vitality and increase the function of harmonizing Qi throughout your whole body. More than ever, you will be able to attune your own Qi to resonate with the universal Qi, to discover the potential of your inner nature, and enjoy living with the force of emptiness while you breathe with the Dao.

2

YAO 藥

THE GREATEST MEDICINE

Grass
Herb
Life

music
Happy
Harmony
Joy

Medicine

Yao Calligraphy in Oracle Bone Script by Master Zhongxian Wu

上藥三品

神與氣精

ShangYaoSanPin ShenYuQiJing

The Greatest Medicine has three varieties, which are Shen, Qi, and Jing

– *YuHuangXinYinMiaoJing* 玉皇心印妙經

You may find that the ancient concept of medicine is drastically different from the modern one. Let's take a look at the Chinese character "Yao 藥" (medicine) to get a feeling for this. The character Yao is composed of two parts: a radical meaning grass or herb on top and the character 樂 for music and joy at bottom. In addition to carrying the meaning of medicine or cure, this Yao character can also stand for music, life force, happiness, and joy. Ancient sages spoke of music as an analogy for universal energy. Harmony is derived from the resonance of sacred sounds. Harmony is also the connection and complementary response of different entities. In other words, the energy created by resonating in harmony with the universe is the original medicine.[1]

Actually, the Yao symbol reveals that anything to be used as medicine must contain these three qualities: life energy, harmony, and joy. Ancient Wu 巫 (Shaman) discovered that Jing 精, Qi 氣, and Shen 神, our own greatest treasures, were the best and most important medicines in the world. Jing, our essential energy, is related to our physical bodies and carries the life energy. Qi, our vital energy, is related to our breathing and delivers harmony. Shen (our spiritual energy) is where the spirit of our bodies is found, and is also linked with the state of our minds and our connection with joy. As the ancients found, our own best medicine resides within our bodies, and practicing a traditional Qigong form like LaoHuGong is the way to access and utilize our Jing, Qi, and Shen.

---

1   Zhongxian Wu, "Dancing and Drumming – Feeling the Rhythm of Qigong, Calligraphy, and Wu (Shamanism)," *Qi: The Journal of Traditional Eastern Health & Fitness*, Winter 2003–2004.

While this access to our Jing, Qi, and Shen medicines alone could be strong enough for any of us on the Daoist healing path, the Tiger further delivers three distinctive, deep acting medicines – Xü, Feng, and Jie – to its dedicated practitioners.

2.1 Xü 虛 – YuanJing 元精 – the Original Essence of the Tiger

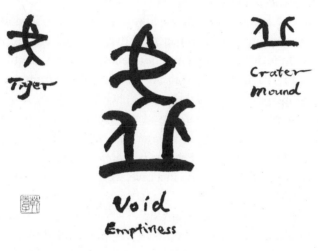

Xü Calligraphy in Oracle Bone Script by Master Zhongxian Wu

道
自
虛
无
生
一
气

DaoZiXüWuShengYiQi

The Dao gives birth to Qi from Xü (Emptiness)

– ZhangBoDuan 張伯端, *WuZhenPian* 悟真篇

The essence of LaoHuGong allows us to cultivate connection with the utmost source of our life power: Xü 虛, or Emptiness. These 24 movements create a direct pathway to experiencing the truth of the Dao. Actually, in classical Qigong 氣功 or NeiDan 內丹 (internal alchemy) practices, in order to approach the highest level of cultivation, enlightenment, we need to LianShenHuanXü 煉神還虛, or refine our Shen (spirit or consciousness) and return to the state of Xü. To help you further understand this concept, I will show how the symbol Xü offers glimpses into the relationship between the power of Hu 虎 (Tiger) and the Daoist concept of the Emptiness.

In general terms, Xü means hollow, void, unreal, and empty. From the Qigong and internal alchemy perspective, the symbolic meanings of Xü also include detachment, emptiness, enlightenment, the birthplace of Qi, and the original of the Dao. As we can imagine from the picture (see Xü calligraphy above) of the ancient JiaGuWen of Xü, the logogram strongly resembles a tiger guarding a cave. We can also perceive this as the image of a tiger running in a crater, or a valley, which suggests the feeling of void or emptiness. Personally, I prefer to see this character as a representation of a tiger living in a cave, which indicates that Xü is the den of the tiger.

Xü is also the name of XiWangMu's 西王母 (Queen Mother of the West[2]) dwelling place, which is one of the most sacred places for Wu 巫 (Chinese shamanism) and Daoism. XiWangMu was a prehistoric matriarchal tribal leader from the period when human beings still lived in caves. Xü is the picture of a cave covered with tiger skin or a tiger's den. It is commonly held that the tiger was one of the most important totems of XiWangMu, where both Xü and tiger were deemed as representations of life energy, justice, and protective Qi for XiWangMu's kingdom and all of her descendants. This concept has widely influenced lives in China (and perhaps some East Asian countries) for ages. For example, even today it is very common for families to hang pictures of the tiger or a tiger talisman in their living room or office as a charm for protection. As mentioned previously, in older times, government officials would commonly use tiger skins to cover their chair in their offices to flaunt their power and righteousness.

---

2   Please read my book *Vital Breath of the Dao* for details about XiWangMu.

In classical Chinese philosophy and cosmology, Xü also represents space and the universe – LiuXü 六虛, or six perspectives of Xü, are the four cardinal directions, above and below. Similar to water, the universal Qi doesn't have a certain shape. As the shape of the container shapes the water within it, different shapes of Xü (or tiger-skin-covered caves) shape the Qi into different patterns that then have different effects on those who live there. The facing direction of tiger skin/cave entrance is influenced by the different qualities held by each directional Xü/universal Qi. The knowledge about the influence of Xü on dwelling space is the earliest evidence of the Daoist art of classical FengShui 風水. Literally translated as wind and water (wind representing Yang Qi and water, Yin Qi), a FengShui master traditionally names a dwelling place Xue 穴, which means hidden cave. A good quality Xue should be able to CangFengJüQi 藏風聚氣 – store the wind and gather Qi. Interestingly, the empty space of Xü is not empty – it generates Qi and fills up with various kinds of Feng 風 (wind, or universal Qi) that affects all lives within. Qi or Feng 風 is the empty force of Xü and represents the symbolic power of tiger.

You may now be wondering: What does FengShui have to do with Qigong and cultivation? The body is both the microcosm, a miniature and complete representation of the macrocosmic universe and the macrocosm, shaping and refining our experience of human culture and shared existence. We influence and are influenced by the Qi flowing in and around us.

Physically, the six main joints – shoulder, hip, elbow, knee, wrist, and ankle, or LiuXü – define the FengShui and flow of Qi within your body. We are able to experience the power of Xü if we learn to unite our Heart-Mind with these six joints during our cultivation practice. LaoHuGong helps create harmonious FengShui within your body, and helps you merge into the Xü state and find your Feng 風 power.

Next, let's take a look at the image of the character, Feng 風.

2.2 Feng 風 – YuanQi 元氣 – the Original Vital Energy of the Tiger

Feng Calligraphy in Oracle Bone Script by Master Zhongxian Wu

風
從
虎

FengCongHu

Winds follow tiger

– *YiJing WenYan* 易經 文言

In Chinese, Feng 風 is actually a complicated word which means much more than "wind." It can be used to signify harmony or harm, grace or scandal, gentle or harsh. The pictograph in oracle bone style looks a bird riding on clouds and Qi, which we can imagine as the representation of the wind currents that support birds in flight. Many scholars and calligraphers favor the idea that the bird symbolized in this character is the phoenix.

In fact, there are deep connections between the two characters Fēng 風 (wind) and Féng 鳳 (phoenix). In spoken Mandarin, both phoenix and wind have very similar pronunciation: Feng. According to the second-century dictionary ShuoWenJieZi 說文解字 and Chinese mythology, the phoenix lives in a place called FengXue 風穴, which literally means wind cave or wind den. As LiuAn 劉安 (179–122 BCE) states in his *HuaiNanZi* 淮南子, HuXiaoErGuFengSheng 虎嘯而谷風生 ("the roar of tiger creates the wind") Feng 風 (wind) is a central symbol of the tiger. Both tiger and phoenix have been the primary totems of XiWangMu and her descendant tribes for thousands of years.

From the above discussion, we understand that tiger generates the wind and phoenix rides with the wind. In other words, phoenix would not be able to fly without tiger.

Phoenix rides on tiger wooden drum from Warrior State period

In traditional Qigong and internal alchemy practices, tiger is a symbol for Qi (or wind) and phoenix is a symbol for Shen (spirit or enlightenment). Through LaoHuGong, you will experience the connection of these two animal symbols. Learning to subdue our inner Tiger is crucial in our Qigong practice, as it is the method through which we achieve transcendence and reach enlightenment.

To give you a little taste of the complexities of the intricacies of the term Feng 風 (wind), the Han Dynasty dictionary, ShuoWenJieZi 說文解字, explains that there are eight different types of wind, comprised of the four cardinal and four diagonal directions, and gives each of them a specific name: East – MingZhe 明庶, Southeast – QingMing 清明, South – Jing 景, Southwest – Liang 涼, West – ChangHe 閶闔, Northwest – BuZhou 不周, North – GuangMo 廣莫, and Northeast – Rong 融. The name and symbolism behind each character of each name provides insight into the energetic qualities of each of these winds. Additionally, in the chapter *JiuGongBaFeng* 九宮八風 of the *HuangDiNeiJing* 黃帝内經 (one of the most important Chinese Medicine classics), these same eight winds are given completely different names: East – YingEr 嬰兒, Southeast – Ruo 弱, South – DaRuo 大弱, Southwest – Mou 謀, West – Gang 剛, Northwest – Zhe 折, North – DaGang 大剛, and Northeast – Xiong 兇. Furthermore, the *HuangDiNeiJing* also draws attention to the specific seasonal relationships to these eight winds and their influences on the different parts of the body. As you can now imagine, Feng 風 (wind) encompasses layers of meaning, permeated with the characteristics of all of its names and manifestations.

Wind symbolizes the Original Vital energy, or YuanQi of the tiger, which is given expression in the BaJie 八節 (Eight Seasons), BaFang 八方 (Eight Directions), and BaGua 八卦 (Eight Trigrams). In traditional Qigong practice, Feng 風 (wind) represents the vital energy Qi in the body. The 24 movements of the Tiger Qigong form allow us to experience and humanize Feng 風 (wind) as it transforms throughout the 24 seasons of the year.

2.3 Jie 節 – YuanShen 元神 – the Original Spirit of the Tiger

Jie Calligraphy in Oracle Bone Script by Master Zhongxian Wu

肺
者
相
傳
之

官
治
節
出
焉

FeiZheXiangFuZhi GuanZhiJieChuYan

The Lung is the prime minister and rules the Jie (rhythm of life)

– HuangDiNeiJing 黃帝內經

The original meaning of Jie 節 is generally believed to be segment, as in the segmented nodes on a piece of bamboo. Examining these segments of bamboo, one notices a pattern or rhythm. In this way, Jie has come to represent rhythm. Other common meanings for Jie are control, rule, adjust, conserve, knot, joint, portion, section, and season.

From the pattern of the ancient oracle bone style, the top character stands for Zhu, bamboo, and the bottom character is typically explained as a person kneeling down next to a dish, which is the symbol for "go to eat." However, from my cultivation perspective, I see the bottom character as a drum on the left with a person on the right, and I interpret the original meaning of Jie as a person using bamboo sticks to beat a drum. This view aligns well with the original meaning of Jie being rhythm. Drumming is one of the most important ancient rituals in Qi cultivation and in connecting human beings with the spiritual world. You will find the rhythm of your own inner drum through the Tiger Qigong practice.

An ancient clay drum excavated from Xia 夏 *Dynasty's ruin site TaoSi* 陶寺 *in ShanXi* 山西 *province, China*

Jie, the fundamental rhythm of nature, symbolizes the divine role of the tiger. In our bodies, the tiger is the spiritual animal of the Lung. Let us take a moment to experience this spirit as it resides in our bodies. Sit at a stable, in a comfortable position with the spine upright (if in a chair, place both feet flat on the floor), and take a deep breath. Can you tell which parts of your body are moving during your deep breath? Yes, the chest! More details, please? Yes, the ribs are moving in the chest. How many ribs are there? There are twelve pairs of ribs in our bodies, totaling 24. The number 24 is the secret number related to our breathing rhythm and to the vital breath of the Dao. As I have mentioned, in nature, the number 24 embodies the rhythm of universal Qi (vital breath of the Dao), also known as ErShiSi JieQi 二十四節氣, or the 24 seasons in an annual cycle.

Traditionally, we apply JieQi to determine the sun's position during each of the 24 seasons and when it occurs during a solar year. This is the fundamental concept of the lunisolar calendar that we Chinese call WanNianLi 萬年曆 or YinYangLi 陰陽曆. WanNianLi translates as "ten thousand years calendar" and YinYangLi means moon and sun calendar, in which case Yin 陰 corresponds to the moon, and Yang 陽,

the sun. In the YinYangLi, each day of the year is specified by the lunar phase and the position of the sun. In other words, in this Chinese calendar, we divide one year into 24 JieQi segments (JieQi is commonly translated as Solar Term or Segment), which are approximately 15 days. The 24 JieQi demarcate the 24 specific sun positions in the sky that make up the 24 major energetic patterns of a year.

The 24 JieQi are formed by twelve Jie 節 and twelve Qi 氣. In this content, Jie means rhythm, segment, or section, and is used to indicate the starting point of an energetic month. Qi means energy, breath, or pulse, and specifies the middle point of the energetic month.

The use of JieQi is essential in understanding various aspects of ancient and modern Chinese culture. In Chinese cosmology and astrology, we use the Jie, the beginning of the energetic month, in order to properly identify the starting point of each energetic month and energetic year. This allows us to assess changing climate patterns or to make predictions using a person's BaZi (Chinese astrology chart) with greater accuracy. In fact, the concept of JieQi was deemed a world treasure on December 1, 2016, when the 24 Solar Terms were given UNESCO's Intangible Cultural Heritage status.

For your convenience, below please find a table briefly summarizing some fundamental associations with the 24 JieQi:

JieQi	Gregorian Date (± 1 day)	Reference for Energetic Month	Meaning	Sun's Ecliptic Longitude
立春 LiChun	Feb 4	1st month initial	Spring begins or establishes	315°
雨水 YuShui	Feb 19	1st month midpoint	Rain water is here	330°
驚蟄 JingZhe	Mar 6	2nd month initial	Hibernators awaken	345°
春分 ChunFen	Mar 21	2nd month midpoint	Mid-spring (vernal equinox)	0°
清明 QingMing	Apr 5	3rd month initial	Time for clearing	15°

cont.

JieQi	Gregorian Date (± 1 day)	Reference for Energetic Month	Meaning	Sun's Ecliptic Longitude
穀雨 GuYu	Apr 20	3rd month midpoint	Grain needs rain	30°
立夏 LiXia	May 6	4th month initial	Summer begins	45°
小滿 XiaoMan	May 21	4th month midpoint	Minor full	60°
芒種 MangZhong	Jun 6	5th month initial	Seeds plump	75°
夏至 XiaZhi	Jun 21	5th month midpoint	Summer peak (solstice)	90°
小暑 XiaoShu	Jul 7	6th month initial	Minor heat	105°
大暑 DaShu	Jul 23	6th month midpoint	Major heat	120°
立秋 LiQiu	Aug 8	7th month initial	Autumn begins	135°
處暑 ChuShu	Aug 23	7th month midpoint	Heat settles down	150°
白露 BaiLu	Sep 8	8th month initial	White dew	165°
秋分 QiuFen	Sep 23	8th month midpoint	Mid-autumn (equinox)	180°
寒露 HanLu	Oct 8	9th month initial	Cold dew	195°
霜降 ShuangJiang	Oct 23	9th month midpoint	Frost descends	210°
立冬 LiDong	Nov 7	10th month initial	Winter begins	225°
小雪 XiaoXue	Nov 22	10th month midpoint	Minor snow	240°
大雪 DaXue	Dec 7	11th month initial	Major snow	255°
冬至 DongZhi	Dec 22	11th month midpoint	Winter peak (solstice)	270°
小寒 XiaoHan	Jan 6	12th month initial	Minor cold	285°
大寒 DaHan	Jan 20	12th month midpoint	Major cold	300°

In Daoist life science, the 24 JieQi are the universal rhythm of the Dao, and from a holistic perspective, they are found in the Lung. Certainly, we can all appreciate that the Lung is in charge of breathing and therefore also regulates the rhythm of Qi. In Chinese medicine, however, the twelve organ systems are symbolized by court positions, and the Lung is considered to be the prime minister of the body. In addition to regulating the rhythm of breath and Qi, the Lung is also charged with being in control of the rhythm of life, including that of our physical movements.

In Chinese, joints are known as GuanJie 関節. A literal translation of this term is "gate node." Our joints, then, become a way to control the rhythms of our body and are intimately connected with universal Qi. If you start to pay close attention to patterns, you may notice that many people with weak Lung function also have joint problems. In Chinese shamanism, the GuanJie are viewed as spiritual gates. There are six major bilateral joints in the body (each with a Yin and Yang aspect): hips, knees, ankles, shoulders, elbows, and wrists, making a total of 24 qualities to consider. The human adult spine, which itself is seen as a spiritual channel, contains 24 separate vertebrae interspaced with cartilage (prior to adolescence, the five bones of the sacrum and four of the coccyx are not yet fused together), each of which is correlated to one JieQi.

In internal alchemy, during the process of transformation, the spine is considered to be the central spiritual channel, allowing the Jing and Qi to move upwards in order to nourish the Shen. During each JieQi period, you will experience more benefits from your cultivation practice if you focus on the appropriately correlated vertebra.

From a classical Chinese Medicine perspective, a person will remain healthy if he or she can maintain ZhengQi in the body. Physically, ZhengQi is most strongly represented by the Lung, which prevents Xie 邪 (evil) Qi from invading the body. In this context, Zheng 正 can be translated as correct or upright. In contrast to Zheng, Xie can be used to describe something that is incorrect or tilted and off-center. Therefore, XieQi includes all factors (e.g. emotions, food, weather, habits, attitude, posture, trauma) that may cause illness. One of the many vital functions of Lung is to govern and energize all the meridians of the body. Practicing correct (Zheng) breathing with the 24 JieQi (as described later, in the LaoHu Gong section of this book) will generate strong Lung Qi, which in turn helps us restore and maintain wellness.

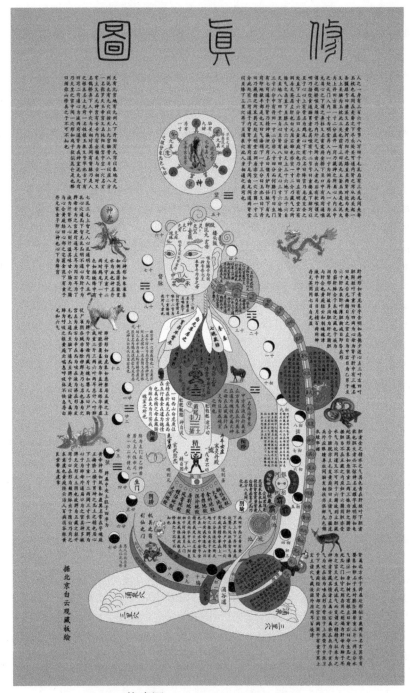

XiuZhenTu 修真圖 – *Daoist internal cultivation diagram*
with 24 JieQi names on their related vertebrae

The reverse is also true: A person will be more susceptible to illness if his or her Lung Qi is weak. There are 24 movements in the Tiger form, which I will share with you later, each of which relate with the seasonal energies of our external and internal milieu, helping move us towards a state of balance and harmony.

3

GEN 根

THE ROOT

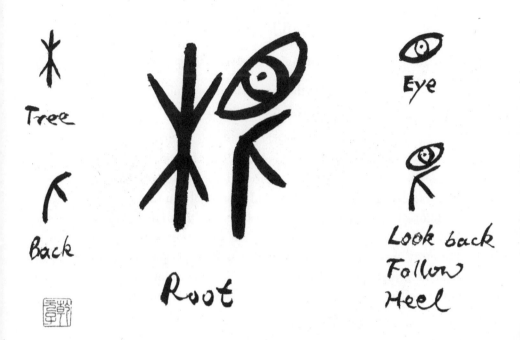

Tree

Back

Root

Eye

Look back
Follow
Heel

Gen Calligraphy in Oracle Bone Script by Master Zhongxian Wu

歸根曰靜
靜謂復命

GuiGenYueJing JingWeiFuMing

Returning to the root is called tranquility;
tranquility is recovering life's fate

– LaoZi 老子, DaoDeJing 道德經 (Chapter 1)

The original meaning of Gen 根 is root. It also commonly means base, foot, radical, reason, completely, and thoroughly. In Chinese wisdom traditions, Gen represents a lineage, root master, the source of a practice, and the source of life. In the higher level of our cultivation practices, the most important and often undisclosed technique is connecting with the lineage and returning to the Gen. In order to connect to the Gen of the LaoHuGong practice, we need to know a little about its lineage.

3.1 EMei ZhenGong 峨嵋真功

LaoHuGong (Chinese Shamanic Tiger Qigong) is from the EMei ZhenGong (Mt. Emei Sage Style Qigong) tradition. The elements of this school are rooted in the ancient world of Wu 巫 (Chinese shamanism), which is the source of all the classical Chinese traditions, such as Confucianism, Daoism, classical Chinese Medicine, traditional Chinese music, *Yijing*, FengShui, and the martial arts. In ancient China, shamans were respected as sages and sages as shamans. The forms' lineage was passed down to me by renowned Chinese medicine doctor, martial artist, and Qigong master Yu WenCai 于文才, from the SiChuan 四川 region of southwest China.

Within the theoretical foundation of Mt. Emei Sage Style Qigong lies the wisdom of ancient *Yijing* science and the principles of classical Chinese Medicine. This Wu 巫 (Chinese shamanic) style is also commonly known as the FuLu 符籙 School. The Chinese character Fu 符

means symbol, omen, in alignment with, and in accord with. Lu 箓 refers to a book of prophecy, an incantation, or a Daoist amulet to ward off evil. The tradition also carries ancient Chinese shamanic rituals, healing arts, internal alchemy, and spiritual cultivation methods that utilize talismans and mantras. Within EMei ZhenGong, we have several teaching systems which each transmit the wisdom of Wu (shamanic) healing and spiritual transformation, Chinese medicine, divination, Qigong, and martial arts.

3.2 Union
– The Primary Attribute of EMei ZhenGong

The most important principle of Mt. Emei Sage Style Qigong is union. This tenet is deeply seated in ancient Chinese civilization. In his book *Peasant Society and Culture*, sociologist Robert Redfield explains that in any civilization both great tradition and little tradition exist. "The great tradition is cultivated in schools or temples; the little tradition works itself out and keeps itself going in the lives of the unlettered in their village communities."[1] The two traditions are interdependent. Mt. Emei Sage Style Qigong, along with other classical systems of Qigong, can be considered a little tradition, whereas Daoism and Confucianism are considered great traditions. The great tradition and the little tradition have long affected each other in China, and acted as the momentum to the development of Chinese civilization. Great or little, the core ideology of all Chinese traditions is union, not separation.

Although many aspects of Chinese culture (music, art, medicine, science, etc.) are commonly attributed to a single great tradition, in truth, traditions are multifaceted, pulling from a variety of sources during their slow development. For instance, *Yijing* (*The Book of Change*) is regarded as the most revered classic of Confucianism. It would be incorrect, however, to think that the *Yijing* is based solely on Confucianism, as most of the practical methods of *Yijing* science, such as Chinese Five Elements astrology, FengShui, and various divination methods, come from Daoism.

---

1   Robert Redfield, *Peasant Society and Culture*. Chicago, IL: University of Chicago Press, 1960, pp.41–45.

Confucianism and Daoism, the two main pillars of classical Chinese tradition, both originated in the ancient world of shamanism. As the way of humanity, Confucianism inherited and rationalized the knowledge of courtesy, ceremonial rites and regulations, and aspects of personal emotion from the ancient shamanic rituals. As the way of nature, Daoism rationalized and expanded the wisdom of the universal way and applied pragmatic knowledge from the ancient shamanic rituals.[2]

Another important classical Chinese tradition is classical Chinese Medicine (CCM). CCM represents the joining of Daoism and Confucianism and is thoroughly based on *Yijing* science. The Tang 唐 Dynasty (617–907 CE) sage Sun SiMiao 孫思邈, who is respected as the "Medicine King" by the Chinese, stated that "nobody qualifies to be a master physician without knowledge of the science of *Yijing*."[3] Indeed, CCM and Chinese shamanism are widely considered to have originated from the same source. In Chinese, the term for this concept is WuYiTongYuan 巫醫同源, which translates literally as "shaman doctor same source." In fact, many ancient documents verify that ancient Chinese doctors were ancient shamans.[4]

We can conclude that shamanism, Confucianism, Daoism, and classical Chinese Medicine interdepend on each other to form a union. Unity itself is the central and most vital common thread that weaves all classical Chinese traditions together. Through the Tiger Qigong form, we will come to see this feature of union and harmony more clearly.

Nota bene: As discussions of unity through the martial arts applications of LaoHuGong are profuse – indeed, enough for a separate book on that topic alone – I will not be addressing them in this book.

2   Li Zehou, *Jimao Wushuo*. Beijing: Zhongguo Dianying Chubanshe, 1999, pp.65–66.

3   Zhang Jiebing, *"Yi yi yi." Leijing Fuyi*. Xian: Shaanxi Kexue Jishu Chubanshe, 1996, p.350.

4   Chen Lai, *Gudai Zongjiao yu Lunli – Lujia Shixiang de Geyuan*. Beijing: Sanlian Shudian, 1996, p.35.

Five Tigers Talisman Calligraphy by Master Zhongxian Wu

4

WU 舞

INNER DANCING
AND DRUMMING

Person
(Standing)

Wield
Wipe out

Dance
Nihility

Wu Calligraphy in Oracle Bone Script by Master Zhongxian Wu

鼓之舞之以盡神

GuZhiWuZhiYiJinShen

Through dancing and drumming, completely connect with the spirit

– Yinjing XiCi 易經繫辭

The oracle bone written pattern of Wu 舞 (dance or dancing) looks like a person doing a powerful Qigong practice, dance, or ritual while in the horse-standing posture. In ancient Wu 巫 (shamanism), dancing is a spiritual ritual. The purpose of dancing is to drive off the devil and connect with the spirit. In my tradition, we carry the essence of the ancient Wu 巫 dance into our Qigong cultivation practice. This core practice is called Shaking, and is also known as the ritual of heart.

An ancient dancing figure from HuaShan 花山 *rock painting in GuangXi* 廣西 *province*

4.1 Dou 抖
– Shake it Up

In the EMei ZhenGong School, when we practice any of the Qigong forms, we typically start with Dou 抖, or shaking Qigong practice. The oracle bone style of the character Dou looks like a hand shaking off dust from a cloth. Shaking is reminiscent of Wu (Chinese shamanic) ceremonial rituals. Ancient Chinese shamans regarded the universal Qi (energy) as a harmonious musical rhythm – the universal vibration. Shaking focuses the body and Shen 神 (spirit) on the universal vibrations we are experiencing. This is a way to break free from stagnation in your physical and spiritual bodies and awaken your vital energy and consciousness.

Most people do not realize that there is a subtle energy – Qi – accompanying them through their entire lives. Some people will never believe the existence of this kind of energy in the body because they have never experienced it. This shaking practice can help us open our spiritual gates and meridians, which are the energy channels in the body. It allows the free flow of Qi to connect with universal energy and thus move the practitioner into a certain level of Qi state.

We can learn to open our hearts to feel the connections between our bodies and nature through our daily practices. Dancing and drumming are shamanic methods of understanding the Shen. Even the shamans of today use the ritual of drumming and dancing to facilitate universal connections, such as bringing rain to dry farmland. In the Chinese shamanic Qigong practice, shaking is the inner dancing and drumming that allows us to access our inner great medicine, harmonize our energetic rhythms to achieve healing, and move towards Enlightenment.

Like shaking, dancing and music are forms of vibration. In my tradition, when we practice Qigong, we always begin with shaking in order to open the pores of our skin to allow universal Qi to come rushing into our bodies, allowing us to connect with the Shen and Qi field of the lineage and lineage masters, and to communicate directly with the universe. During the shaking practice, we use different sounds or mantras to open the meridians and all the cells of the body, in order to resonate with the universal energies and harmonize with the universal Qi. This process in Qigong is no different from the Wu rituals of dancing and drumming – through vibrations and special frequencies, Wu connect with the universal Qi, their own spirits, and high-level beings.

4.2 Zhen 震
– Awaken Your Qi, Awaken Your Consciousness

We are going to start the practice of shaking. The practice is correlated with the *Yijing* trigram Zhen 震, which has one solid line at the bottom and two broken lines on top. The Chinese character Zhen 震 means shake, vibration, or move. Thunder represents this quality of shaking; it is the vibration of the world, shaking. From a Chinese shamanic perspective, roaring thunder is the spirit of Nature that wakes up all beings and creates "new-life" energy. Shaking Qigong is also a way to help you rejuvenate your own new-life energy.

Step 1

In a standing position, bring your feet together, maintaining contact with the ground. Keep your body erect, arms hanging loosely by your sides with your fingers pointing downwards. Imagine tennis balls in your armpits. Your chin is slightly lowered. Close your eyes, placing the tip of your tongue against the roof of your mouth, just behind your teeth.

Visualize yourself stretching – the top of your head and spine reaches up into the Heavens while your feet grow roots that anchor deeply into Earth. See your arms extending downwards with your fingertips reaching the center of the Earth. Pull Earthly YinQi 陰氣 from the center of the Earth and feel it filling your whole body.

See the sun and moon. See the Big Dipper. From the Big Dipper, find the North Star and feel the connection between the North Star and the BaiHui 百會 (100 meetings) point (GV 20) on the crown of your head. Feel the universal Qi pouring into your body through the BaiHui point and filling up your whole body with the heavenly YangQi 陽氣. See the planets and feel yourself connecting with each of them. Concentrate on your DanTian 丹田 and see it as a small sun or ball of fire in your lower abdomen.

Step 2

Step to the right, feet shoulder-width apart. Raise up onto your toes and hold yourself there. Jump. When you land, start shaking your whole body, bouncing rhythmically, all the while breathing into the DanTian and making the mantra Heng 哼 (pronounced "Hung") with each breath. Bring the lineage and universal Qi into all the pores of your body. Make the mantra Heng on each out-breath to concentrate Qi in the lower DanTian. As you move faster and faster, the ball/sun of your DanTian becomes denser and denser.

As you continue shaking, think of the body parts successively:

First think about the Heavenly Gate (BaiHui). Open this gate further to receive Heavenly Qi.

Then think about shaking each eye, your nose, mouth, face, ears, neck, shoulders, arms, elbows, wrists, fingers, chest, heart, Lungs, spleen, stomach, pancreas, bladder, liver, gall bladder, intestines, pelvic organs, spine, hips, legs, knees, ankles, and feet.

Then shake your whole body in a freestyle manner.

Gradually slow down and then come to a complete stop. Gather the heavenly Qi over the crown of your head and then bring it with open hands, palm facing down, down the front-center of your body, stopping with palms facing your lower DanTian. Relax. Feel the tingling. Feel the warmth. Feel the heat. Feel the light entering and nourishing your whole body, as if you are taking a Qi shower. Then move your consciousness to your lower DanTian and concentrate the energy there. Observe the inner landscape of your body with your inner eye. At this moment, you may have special experiences in your body and spirit. Observe your body. Observe your inner landscape.

5

FA 灋

THE WAY OF SHAMANIC TIGER QIGONG

Water

Way
Law
Rule

Deer
ELK
Moose

Fa Calligraphy in Oracle Bone Script by Master Zhongxian Wu

五虎將

畫虎虎

己亥夏
乾元子

DaoFaZiRan

The Dao follows its natural way

– LaoZi 老子, *DaoDeJing* 道德經 (Chapter 1)

In this section, we will learn the methods of correctly practicing LaoHuGong. The learning method is called Fa 灋 in Chinese. From the oracle bone configuration of Fa, we see that it looks a deer-type animal walking towards the water. This character reveals that the ancient Wu (shaman) emphasized that a learning technique should follow the way of nature. This Qigong form itself models the rhythm of nature, coinciding with the rhythm of the four seasons and 24 JieQi. Therefore, I will divide the practice in four parts. In the beginning of each section, I will add a quotation from the *HuangDiNeiJing* 黃帝內經, one of the most important Chinese Medicine classics, to help you better understand the movements and how they relate to seasonal influences.

Spring Tiger

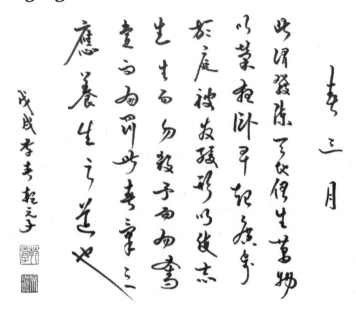

Spring Quotation Calligraphy by Master Zhongxian Wu

養　此　賞　予　生　以　被　廣　夜　萬　天　此　春
生　春　而　而　而　使　髮　步　臥　物　地　謂　三
之　氣　勿　勿　勿　志　緩　於　早　以　俱　發　月
道　之　罰　奪　殺　生　形　庭　起　榮　生　陳
也　應

ChunSanYue, CiWeiFaChen, TianDiJuSheng, WanWuYiRong,
YeWoZaoQi, GuangBuYuTing, PiFaHuanXing,
YiShiZhiSheng, ShengErWuSha, YuErWuDuo, ShangErWuFa,
CiChunQiZhiYing, YangShengZhiDaoYe.

The three months of spring season are called FaChen 發陳 ["release old energy"]. Both Heaven and Earth generate new-life energies during this season – everything is flourishing. Go to bed when it is dark and get up early, widen your steps and walk about in your yard. Loosen your hair and be gentle with your body to uplift your spirit. Compassion over violence, giving without taking, appreciate instead of punish. Above all, resonate with the spring Qi, the Dao of generating your new-life energy.

5.1   HongMengYiQi 鴻蒙一炁 – Return to the Great Primordial Qi

Meaning: Hong means great, big, and vast. **Meng** means unknown, vague, moistening. **Meng** is also the name of Hexagram Four of the *Yijing*, Mountain over Water. This hexagram is an image of a fresh spring at the foot of the mountain. It is a good Qi field in which to live and grow. The function of **Meng** is to nourish and create ZhengQi 正氣 (righteous Qi). "The Superior Person refines his or her character by being thorough in every activity," according to the *Yijing*, which indicates not only that this Qigong cultivation method should be part of daily life, but also that we can apply the essential technique of this movement in every activity of life. **Meng** can also mean unclear, enshrouded in fog and moisture. **Yi** means One, the state of oneness of the universe. **Qi** is the vital energy or breath. In terms of Chinese cosmology, in the beginning, the primordial universe was one big ball of Qi.

The Tiger form is patterned after the rhythm of universal Qi. According to *Yijing* principles, Heaven is classified as Metal Qi and during this first movement in the Tiger form we connect with Metal Qi, or primordial life energy. In other words, we move into a state of unity with primordial universe state, where all is one. **HongMengYiQi**, then, means return to the primordial or original state of the universe.

JieQi 節氣: This movement is associated with LiChun 立春 (Spring begins). As the first JieQi of a year, it is the starting point of the Tiger month (the first month), spring season, and a new Chinese animal year (which represents start of the energetic year). It denotes the beginning of a new life. Resonating with this seasonal energy through this opening movement of the Tiger form will help regenerate your new-life energy.

JingMai 經脈 (Meridians and Channels): Of the twelve organ meridians, this movement is linked with the ShouTaiYinFeiJing 手太陰肺經 (Hand Great Yin Lung Meridian). Of the eight extraordinary channels, the movement is connected with YangQiaoMai 陽蹻脈 (Yang Bridge Channel). This indicates that when practiced often, the movement will improve your Lung function, clear heat, balance your blood pressure, and improve the quality of your sleep.

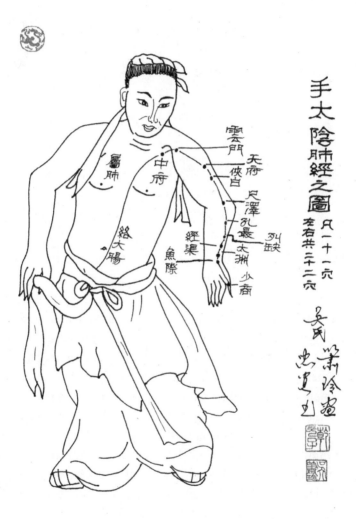

Lung Meridian

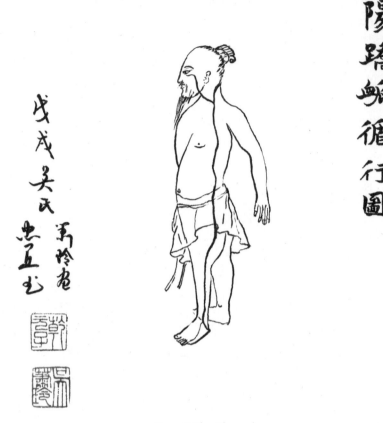

Yang Bridge Channel

Movement: Stand with your feet together and toes grabbing the Earth. Straighten your back so it is as stable as a mountain. Lift your perineum to seal DiHu 地户 (Earthly Door, CV 1). Tuck the lower abdomen in, slightly. Open your chest. Straighten your neck and keep your head upright. Imagine your head touching Heaven with the TianMen 天門 (Heavenly Gate, GV 20) remaining open. Place the tip of your tongue on the tooth ridge behind your upper teeth. Keep your teeth held together and your mouth closed. Keep your shoulders down, arms relaxed, and armpits just slightly open. Relax your hands and keep your fingers straight. Relax your eyelids. Bring your eyesight within. Look within. Listen within. Visualize and sense the Qi state.

Visualization: With your eyelids relaxed, look and listen within to visualize the Qi state. Visualize yourself stretching – the top of your head and spine reach up into the Heavens while your feet grow roots that anchor deeply into Earth. Feel the Heavenly and Earthly energies penetrate to mix in the DanTian. Imagine the universal Qi as light surrounding your body. Open all the pores of the skin, allowing the universal Qi to pour into your body. Feel your body merging with the Qi and returning to the state of primordial universe Qi.

Breathing: Breathe through your nose. Breathe through your skin. Adjust your breathing to be slow, smooth, deep, and even. There should be no noise from your breathing. In Chinese, this breathing technique is called MiMiMianMian 密密綿綿, meaning the breathing is soft and unbroken, like cotton and silk. Gather the Qi with all the pores of your body as you inhale. Condense the Qi in your DanTian 丹田 as you exhale.

Function: This movement appears to do nothing, but it is actually doing a great deal. It is a way to help you awaken to the original life source and it is creating and nourishing ZhengQi 正气. This movement opens the body and enables us to connect with universal Qi. It also helps us learn about the union of the physical body and the spiritual body. Daily practice of the movement strengthens the vital energy and is good for rebuilding one's life energy after a period of weakness.

5.2 ShuiHuJueXing 睡虎覺醒 – Sleeping Tiger Wakes Up

Meaning: Shui means sleep, unknown. **Hu** means tiger. In Chinese, another name for tiger is DaChong 大虫, which literally means big or great worm. As surprising as it first sounds, there is actually a symbolic connection between the tiger and the worm. The symbolic meaning of worm in Chinese shamanism is strong life energy, and absence of stagnation. This strong life energy is apparent when we cut a worm in half. Not only can it still move, but it can regenerate itself into two worms. **Jue** means feel, sense, aware, sight, observe, wisdom, and Enlightenment. **Xing** means to wake up. **ShuiHu**, a sleeping tiger, is a symbol for an unenlightened person. Everyone has the capacity to be enlightened. However, a person may never discover this capacity and cultivate it if his or her consciousness is buried in the business and distractions of everyday life. This movement, which imitates a tiger waking up, represents the awakening of our deepest consciousness and the latent potential residing in the body. Through practice and discipline – daily cultivation – we work with the three treasures, the best medicine in the body: Jing (Essence), Qi (Vital energy), and Shen (Spirit). This movement teaches us that the original purpose of Qigong practice is as a way of achieving Enlightenment.

JieQi 節氣: This movement is associated with YuShui 雨水 (Rain water is here). The second JieQi of a year, it is the midpoint of the Tiger month (first month). It represents a nourishing stage of life. Practicing this movement of the Tiger form will help you resonate with this seasonal energy, and help awaken your life energy and nourish your joints (your spiritual fortress).

JingMai 經脈 (Meridians and Channels): As with the previous movement, of the twelve organ meridians, this movement is linked with the ShouTaiYinFeiJing 手太陰肺經 (Hand Great Yin Lung Meridian, see Section 5.1), and of the eight extraordinary channels, the movement is connected with YangQiaoMai 陽蹻脈 (Yang Bridge Channel, see Section 5.1). As with the previous movement, this indicates that when practiced often, the movement will also help improve your Lung function, clear heat, balance your blood pressure, and improve your quality of sleep.

Movement: Feel the weight and power of the tiger's bones and muscles – your bones and muscles. Your fingers should be curled like tiger claws as your hands move. This is important for holding the energy. The acupuncture points on the extremities are located on the tips of your fingers and toes, the border where microcosmic energy meets macrocosmic energy. Move your whole body, including your legs, and feel yourself undulate with the martial power of the tiger. When you feel you have become the tiger, the whole body will surge from the DanTian. Make sure that your toes are always grabbing the floor. Move your arms like waves, with fingers curled into tiger claws. Tiger looks heavy but moves fast. The tiger is very sensitive and agile.

Visualization: Imagine you are a tiger waking up from a deep sleep. Begin connecting with the energy of the tiger. Become the tiger. Feel the joints of the body opening. Feel the whole body moving freely without stagnation, moving like a worm.

Breathing: Regulate your breath as you did in the first movement and start moving your body. Then modify your breathing to imitate a tiger yawning. Take a deep breath and make a soft growling noise like a tiger.

Function: This movement releases Qi stagnation and strengthens the Liver function, improving the flexibility of the whole body. It helps us to awaken and to understand the energy in our deeper layers – that energy which is usually never accessed or used by the conscious mind. By doing this form, we will become deeply aware of the presence of the special treasures of the body: Jing, Qi, and Shen.

5.3   LiDiBaiWei 立地擺尾
– Tiger Wags Its Tail

Meaning: Li means standing, establish. **Di** means Earth. **LiDi** means standing on the Earth or building up the Earth energy in the body. It is a symbol of being rooted. Our cultivation practice needs to be grounded. The state of being grounded is another symbolic meaning of the tiger. The tiger is a symbol of status and also carries the meaning of knowing one's rank, place, and position. Although the tiger is powerful when moving, he is most often found "sitting in place," "dwelling at home," or "presiding from his lair" while surveying his kingdom, acutely aware of everything going on below. Learning "who I am" and "where I will be" (i.e. location and position) will help us ground. We need to be in the moment and we need to connect with life around us. Remember how I told you that the pattern of the tiger skin also represents the Dao? In other words, the Dao is very close – life and spiritual cultivation should not be separated. **BaiWei** means wagging the tail. The tail represents the power of the tiger – it is from here that the tiger derives its power. **BaiWei** is a symbol for pride. The acts of practice and cultivation are venerable, and we can be proud of their presence in our lives.

JieQi 節氣: This movement is associated with JingZhe 驚蟄 (Hibernators awaken). The third JieQi of a year, it is the starting point of the Rabbit month (second month) and the mid-spring season. It represents the awakening of consciousness. Practicing this movement of the Tiger form will help you resonate with this seasonal energy and help lift your spirit and awaken your consciousness.

JingMai 經脈 **(Meridians and Channels):** Of the twelve organs meridians, this movement is associated with the ShouYangMingDaChangJing 手陽明大腸經 (Hand Yang Brightness Large Intestine Meridian). Of the eight extraordinary channels, the movement is connected with YangQiaoMai 陽蹻脈 (Yang Bridge Channel, see Section 5.1). This indicates that when practiced often, the movement will improve your digestive and large intestine function, detoxification pathways, and improve the quality of your sleep.

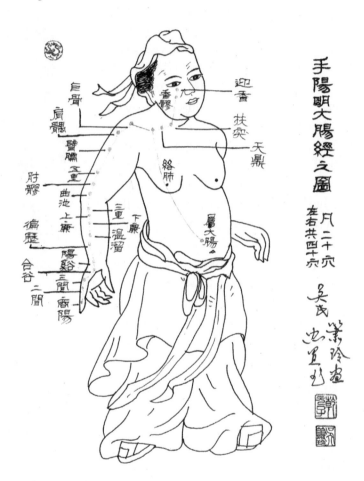

II. Hand Yangming Large Intestine Meridian

Large Intestine Meridian

Movement: As you breathe in, take a step to the right and make a wide horse stance. Bring your left hand up, palm facing right, with the thumb in front of your mouth, as your right hand swings behind you, palm facing left, with thumb in front of your tailbone. Straighten your arms and pay attention to the palms. Be sure they are in the center-line of your body. Focus on your tailbone. The tailbone is the end of the spine and is the secret source of our life power. Breathe out and shake your tailbone. Allow your body to move with your tailbone. Repeat this sequence of shaking on this side five times. Five is an Earth number and represents the Five Elements. After repeating the sequence five times, switch arms and do the same movement on the other side. Do three rounds of this movement. Three is the number of creation, and symbolizes the three layers: Heaven, Earth, and the Human Being. Together, these three layers represent the universe.

Visualization: Imagine you are the tiger standing with feet rooting into the Earth. Wag the tail, focusing on the tailbone as you wag your hips. Feel the momentum from your tiger tailbone.

Breathing: Take a deep, sharp breath before shaking the tailbone. Then breathe out with the mantra Heng 哼 (pronounced "Hung") as you are shaking.

Function: This movement enhances the ZhongQi 中氣, the central energy of the body, and calls upon Earth element energy and its harmonizing function. It is good for any digestive or Earth-related pathology. Since Earth (Tu 土) is the mother of Metal (Jin 金), it is logical to begin with the root of Metal in this form. This movement is a way to build up your Earth energy (physical health, mental stability, and harmonizing function) before we play with the Metal animal, Tiger.

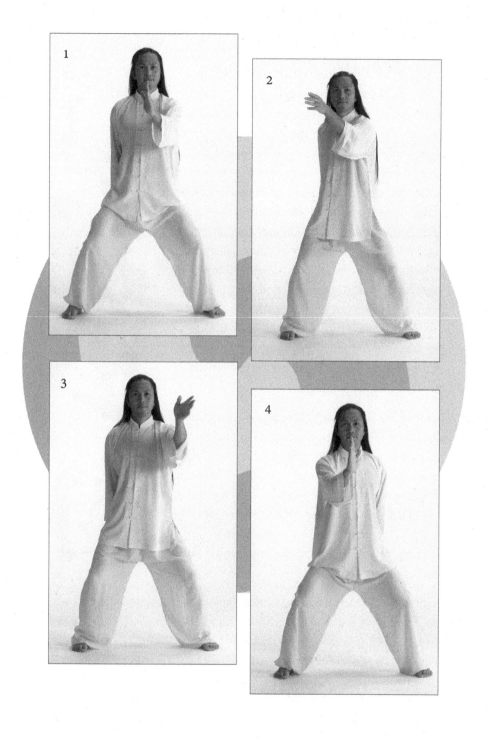

5.4 DanDanChuDong 眈眈出洞 – Tiger Emerges from the Cave

Meaning: DanDan means glare, gaze, stare. Eyes represent the spiritual windows of the soul. When we start our practice, we are opening the spiritual windows to connect with the outer world and to learn the universal way. This movement is the pattern of the tiger's eyes – open and staring fiercely. **Chu** means come out, emerge. **Dong** means cave – the tiger's home and also the first home of our ancestors. Tiger is the epitome of the wild animal, displaying powerful survival instincts and a need for freedom. Tiger needs "breathing space" and the freedom to roam and defend vast territories. This movement is a symbol for open space or an open heart. In Qigong practice, one can learn how to open the spiritual windows of the Heart-Mind, not merely remain in the small cave of our familiar existence.

JieQi 節氣: This movement is associated with ChunFen 春分 (Vernal Equinox). The fourth JieQi of a year, it is the midpoint of the Rabbit month (second month) and the midpoint of spring season. It represents the balance of Yin and Yang. Practicing this movement of the Tiger form will help you resonate with this seasonal energy and will help you bring balance to your whole body and to your life in general.

JingMai 經脈 (Meridians and Channels): Of the twelve organ meridians, this movement is associated with the ShouYangMingDaChangJing 手陽明大腸經 (Hand Yang Brightness Large Intestine Meridian, see Section 5.3). Of the eight extraordinary channels, the movement is connected with ChongMai 衝脈 (Vigor Channel). This indicates that when practiced often, the movement will improve your large intestine function, detoxification pathways, blood circulation, and increase your sexual energy.

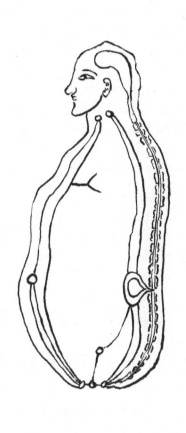

衝脈循行圖

Vigor Channel

Movement: Ending with your right hand out in front of you after the third round of "Tiger Wags its Tail," slowly rotate your right hand so the palm faces right while you sweep your right arm out to the side, and, in a continuous movement, bend your right elbow and begin to rotate your wrist and elbow so that the right hand moves forward to a 90-degree angle in front of your body, at chest level. The right palm is facing Heaven. Simultaneously, bring your left arm around from behind, rotating your left palm down and bringing it to rest in front of you. The right arm will pass over your left arm, eventually ending with your left hand, palm facing Earth, under your right elbow. All of this is done as you are pivoting to the left. The arms cooperate with each other, creating a Yin-Yang movement. Explore your territory, working the meridians in your arms and feeling the energy. The energy from your right hand and fingers should be penetrating and shooting outward.

Visualization: Extend your fingers far away and feel your fingers touch the ends of the universe. Feel the LaoGong 勞宮 (Palace of Weariness, PC 8) of your upper hand connect with Heaven as you feel the LaoGong of your lower hand connect with Earth. Be aware of your eyesight perceiving the outside world, seeing far away and taking in everything in the universe.

Breathing: Regulate your breath with the lower DanTian. Inhale and exhale, feeling the Qi rotate in your lower DanTian. Visualize the breath in your lower DanTian as a moving Qi ball, picturing the Taiji symbol for energy circulation.

Function: This movement helps open the four largest spiritual gates in the body: the two hips and the two shoulders. By circulating the energy in the lower DanTian, the energy of the body unites with universal energy. This moves us from separation into unification. The movement is good for Heart function or any disease of the limbs.

5.5   YaoWuYangWei 耀武揚威 – Tiger Displays Martial Power

Meaning: Yao means shining, lightning, show, and display. **Wu** means martial power. Thus, **YaoWu** means to display one's martial power. **Yang** means show, wave. **Wei** means respect, venerable, or spiritual power. It is a sincere feeling of respect for nature and for our practice. In the traditional way, doing Qigong practice is like performing a special ceremony or ritual to connect oneself with the universe. The tiger displaying its martial power represents us bringing out our inner potential for spiritual power. This is a special type of spiritual energy that one uses for cultivation. In our Qigong practice, new challenges are met often, and we need this inner power to feel confident and determined.

JieQi 節氣: This movement is associated with QingMing 清明 (Time for clearing). The fifth JieQi of a year, it is the beginning point of the Dragon month (third month) and the last spring month. It represents the importance of purification and connection with the ancestral spirits. Practicing this movement of the Tiger form will help you resonate with this seasonal energy and will help you release blockages in your body as well as rejuvenate your life source.

JingMai 經脈 (Meridians and Channels): Of the twelve organ meridians, this movement is aligned with the ZuYangMingWeiJing 足陽明胃經 (Foot Yang Brightness Stomach Meridian). Of the eight extraordinary channels, the movement is connected with ChongMai 衝脈 (Vigor Channel, see Section 5.4). This indicates that when practiced often, the movement will improve your digestive function, keep you feeling young, and increase your sexual energy.

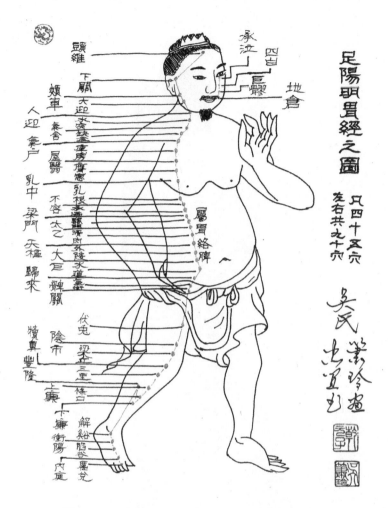

III. Foot Yangming Stomach Meridian

Stomach Meridian

Movement: Pivot in a slow, relaxed fashion back to the right, suddenly snapping your right wrist so that your right palm, facing forward, is more upward and slightly higher than eye level. Allow your left hand to move down to face the lower DanTian and connect with Earthly Qi. Work the meridians in your arms and legs, twisting and undulating your wrists, arms, shoulders, hips, and legs – feeling the power and strength of the tiger. Feel your Qi move through all parts of your tiger body, even to the tips of each hair on your body.

Visualization: Imagine being a dragon. Feel your whole body move – not just the wrists and hands. Your whole body spirals, and the Qi condenses into the bone and marrow (QiLianRuGu 气敛入骨). At the same time, feel as if each hair on the body is like a needle or an iron weapon standing straight up.

Breathing: Allow your breath to be slow, smooth, deep, and even. Breathe with all the pores of your skin, not with just the Lungs. Occasionally, you can make a slow inhale followed by a sharp exhale with the mantra, Heng 哼.

Function: This movement connects us with the harmony of universal Qi and is excellent for dispersing Qi stagnation in the body. It also helps strengthen Kidney and Liver Qi and harmonizes Lung and Liver Qi.

5.6   ShenJianZhanXie 神劍斬邪 – Spiritual Sword Kills the Demon

Meaning: Shen means spirit, divine, essence. **Jian** is a sword, which is a symbol for wisdom. **Zhan** means cut off with a sharp motion, chop. **Xie** means evil (as in Xie Qi), devil, demon, ghost. **Xie** also means all the factors that cause illness – it may be a blockage in your body, problems in your life, unbalanced emotions, or anything that pulls you away from or blocks you from your endeavors. In our Qigong practice, we always feel resistance – this is the evil Qi that makes us feel that it is all right not to practice. If we don't have wisdom, we follow this "outside face," which is beautiful and alluring but keeps us from moving forward. The spiritual sword represents the special wisdom we need for cutting off the influence of evil energy. Through practice, we will become stronger physically, emotionally, and spiritually. We must develop the ability to kill the inner demons that prevent us from moving into a better state. The symbolic meaning of this movement is that through the kill, a new spiritual life will be born.

JieQi 節氣: This movement is associated with GuYu 谷雨 (Grain needs rain). The sixth JieQi of a year, it is the midpoint of the Dragon month (third month) and the last spring month. It represents the importance of spiritual cultivation necessities. In Chinese wisdom traditions, in order to achieve enlightenment, you must have four supplies: Fa 灋 (methods which lead you to the Dao), Cai 財 (finances to support you on your journey), Lü 侶 (harmonious spiritual companions), Di 地 (a good FengShui environment). Practicing this movement of the Tiger form will help you resonate with this seasonal energy and will help you work with the four cultivation necessities so that you will reach the goal of spiritual transformation.

JingMai 經脈 **(Meridians and Channels):** Of the twelve organ meridians, this movement is affiliated with the ZuYangMingWeiJing 足陽明胃經 (Foot Yang Brightness Stomach Meridian, see Section 5.5). Of the eight extraordinary channels, the movement is connected with ChongMai 衝脈 (Vigor Channel, see Section 5.4). As with the previous movement, this indicates that when practiced often, the movement will improve your digestive function, keep you feeling young, and increase your sexual energy.

Movement: Turn your whole body slowly 180 degrees, back to the left. Keeping your feet firmly planted when you pivot, your right hand floats up above your head, stirring the heavens. Your left hand remains at the level of your DanTian. Then cross your arms by slicing your right hand downward suddenly like a cosmic sword full of Qi to a position below your waist on the opposite side, as your left elbow bends and left hand comes up to the right side of your chin with the palm facing out, to guard.

Visualization: Imagine that your hands and arms are the sword – sharp, hard, righteous metal. When the hands cross, they move in a scissoring action, as if two swords are cooperating to release everything created from the old evil energy. Envision driving off evil energy. The "fight" here is not with another entity, but with the ego residing deep within our heart. The practice helps us recognize and drive away the "evil" hidden inside our own heart. It is important to understand that this tendency exists in all of us. Merely following our feelings does not always lead us down the right path.

Breathing: Inhale as your arms open. As your arms cross, exhale. At the end of your exhale, make the Heng mantra, but with your mouth closed. You can do two or three Heng mantras in quick succession.

Function: This movement benefits the shoulders. It can help release a frozen shoulder or other shoulder conditions. It is also a way to strengthen your healing power and your ability to transmit external Qi. You can use this movement to help drive off any kind of disease. The Heng mantra has the function of releasing evil Qi, with or without the body movement. It is especially good for the Heart and Shen.

Summer Tiger

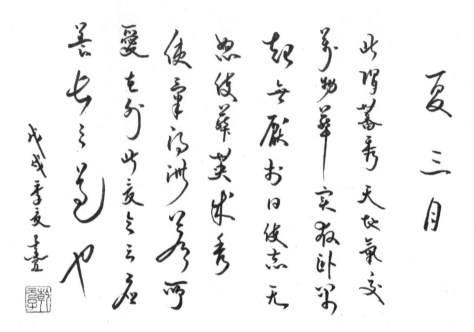

Summer Quotation Calligraphy by Master Zhongxian Wu

夏
三
月

此
謂
蕃
秀

天
地
氣
交

萬
物
華
實

夜
臥
早
起

無
厭
於
日

使
志
無
怒

使
華
英
成
秀

使
氣
得
泄

若
所
愛
在
外

此
夏
氣
之
應

養
長
之
道
也

XiaSanYue, CiWeiFanXiu, TianDiQiJiao, WanWuHuaShi, YeWoZaoQi, WuYanYuRi, ShiZhiWuNu, ShiHuaYingChengXiu, ShiQiDeXie, RuoSuoAiZaiWai, CiXiaQiZhiYing, YangZhangZhiDaoYe

The three months of summer season are called FanXiu 蕃秀, which means producing elegance. In this season, the Qi of Heaven and Earth coalesce and everything is blossoming and fruitful. Go to bed when it is dark and get up early. Do not complain about your day, control your temper, and transform your talents into your bounty. Activities release your energy, especially those you pour your full heart into. Above all, resonate with the summer Qi – the Dao of expanding your life energy.

5.7   QiHuaSanPan 气化三盤 – Qi Transforms the Three Layers

Meaning: Qi is the vital energy of nature. **Hua** means change or transformation. It is any process that changes matter from one state to another, like the worm (caterpillar) transforming into the butterfly. In Qigong practice, **QiHua** refers to Qi removing blockages to allow the energy to flow. This is a cultivated Qi healing skill. After dedicating yourself to your Qigong practice for a certain period of time (the amount of time varies individually), you may use your Qi to transform your own areas of Qi stagnation or to transform another person's, to help promote healing, flowing Qi. **San** means three. **Pan** means plate, layer, or circle. It also means something that is coiled together. **SanPan** means the three layers. In Chinese wisdom traditions, the three layers have many symbolic meanings. In the body, they relate to the three parts of the body (upper, middle, lower). In terms of energy, they refer to the Jing, Qi, and Shen. In terms of the universe, they refer to Heaven, Earth, and Humanity. All three layers connect with the flow of Qi. Thus, this movement of the Tiger form helps the Qi flow smoothly in the three layers in such a way that peace and harmony is experienced.

JieQi 節氣: This movement is related to LiXia 立夏 (Summer begins). The seventh JieQi of a year, it is the beginning point of the Snake month (fourth month) and the first summer month. It represents maturation. Practicing this movement of the Tiger form will help you resonate with this seasonal energy and will help you find your inner strength.

JingMai 經脈 (**Meridians and Channels**): Of the twelve organ meridians, this movement is connected with the ZuTaiYinPiJing 足太陰脾經

(Foot Great Yin Spleen Meridian). Of the eight extraordinary channels, the movement is linked with YinWeiMai 陰維脈 (Yin Safeguard Channel). This indicates that when practiced often, the movement will improve your digestive function and your spleen Qi, and strengthen your heart.

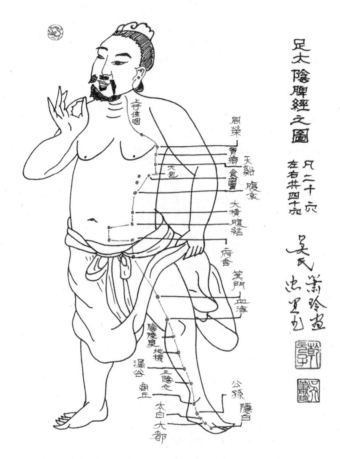

IV. Foot Taiyin Spleen Meridian

Spleen Meridian

Movement: Rotate back to center, bringing your right arm up as you turn the palm down and turn your left palm up until they meet at head level with your left hand resting under your right elbow. Feel yourself holding a Qi ball with your palms. Rotate left and right with your arms, turning your palms over with each shift in direction. Rotate the upper body once at the upper DanTian, once at the middle DanTian and once at the lower DanTian. This represents the harmonizing of Heaven, Earth, and the Human Being.

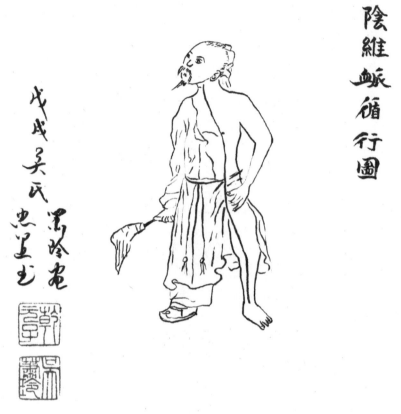

Yin Safeguard Channel

Visualization: Visualize holding a ball of Qi with both hands. Imagine extending your fingers to touch the ends of the universe. As your hands move, visualize the Qi following the hands and passing through the three layers of Heaven, Earth, and Humanity. Envision cooperation between all three DanTian.

Breathing: Inhale deeply before shifting right. Exhale as you shift right. Inhale as you shift left.

Function: This movement transforms physical blockages and stagnation, which allows the Qi to flow smoothly. It balances the three burners in the body (upper, middle, and lower), which are equivalent to the three layers, Heaven, Earth, and the Human Being. Diseases that are related to the three burners include heart and Lung diseases, gastrointestinal disease, and kidney disease. Diseases located in these areas may manifest in insomnia, anxiety, chest pain, nausea, and low back pain. In addition, this movement also strengthens the ability to transmit external Qi for healing.

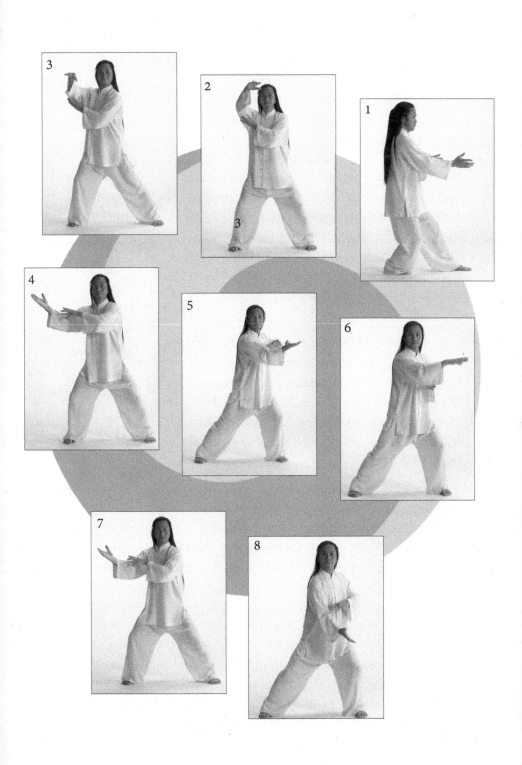

5.8   TongTianCheDi 通天徹地 – Connect with Heaven and Penetrate Earth

Meaning: Tong means connect, communicate, pathway, flowing, circulation. **Tian** means Heaven. **Che** means penetrate, complete, perfect. **Di** means Earth. **TongTianCheDi** is the ability to connect with the universe. As ancient Chinese shamans had the ability to connect with the universe through ritual and practice, we too have the potential to connect with universal energy. This is the experience of ultimate freedom in Qigong practice – through our cultivation, we can learn to harmonize our energy with nature.

JieQi 節氣: This movement is related to XiaMan 小滿 (Minor Full). The eighth JieQi of a year, it is the midpoint of the Snake month (fourth month) and the first summer month. It represents the maturity of young adults. Practicing this movement of the Tiger form will help you resonate with this seasonal energy and will help you find self-confidence.

JingMai 經脈 **(Meridians and Channels):** Of the twelve organ meridians, this movement is connected with the ZuTaiYinPiJing 足太陰脾經 (Foot Great Yin Spleen Meridian, see Section 5.7). Of the eight extraordinary channels, the movement is linked with YinWeiMai 陰維脈 (Yin Safeguard Channel, see Section 5.7). As with the previous movement, this indicates that when practiced often, the movement will improve your digestive function, spleen Qi, and strengthen your heart.

Movement: After finishing the third round of harmonizing the three layers, shift your body back to the center. Quickly snap your right wrist out and upward with palm up to Heaven (above BaiHui, GV 20) as you snap your left hand with palm down and at the level of your lower

DanTian. Move your hands in a slight rotational movement so that you feel the connection between Heaven and Earth.

Visualization: Visualize your fingertips and LaoGong of the right hand connecting with Heaven. The fingertips of the left hand root into and connect with the deepest layers of Earth. Extend yourself, both physically and spiritually. Feel the whole body expanding like a dragon to connect with Heaven and Earth.

Breathing: Allow your breath to be slow, smooth, deep, and even.

Function: This movement can help strengthen our ability to connect with universal energy. It is also a helpful way to open the different layers of the body. This movement will enhance the sensitivity in your fingers and LaoGong so that you may receive and transmit external Qi. It is beneficial for Triple Burner and digestion function.

5.9   HuaiBaoRiYue 懷抱日月 – Embrace the Sun and Moon

Meaning: Huai means chest, hold, and heart.
Bao means embrace, hug. **Ri** 日 is the sun. **Yue**
月 is the moon. The Chinese character formed
by combining the characters for sun and moon
is Ming 明, which means brightness, light,
Enlightenment. The symbol on the left side of the
radical, Sun, is Yang in energy and the one on the
right side of the radical, Moon, is Yin. Sun and
moon together mean brightness – the brightness
of the Heart that is enlightened. The traditional
belief is that the heart of an enlightened being is
big enough to hold the sun and moon. The heart
also holds the spirit or Shen Ming 神明 – the
spiritual light. This movement symbolizes the
Heart as the residence or palace of the Dao within
the body.

JieQi 節氣: This movement is related to
MangZhong 芒種 (Seeds plump). The ninth JieQi
of a year, it is the beginning point of the Horse
month (fifth month) and the middle summer
month. It represents the development of glorious
life. Practicing this movement of the Tiger form
will help you resonate with this seasonal energy
and will help you find your inner wisdom.

JingMai 經脈 (**Meridians and Channels**): Of
the twelve organ meridians, this movement is
connected with the ShouShaoYinXinJing 手少
陰心經 (Hand Less Yin Heart Meridian). In the eight extraordinary
channels, the movement is linked with YinWeiMai 陰維脈 (Yin
Safeguard Channel, see Section 5.7). This indicates that when practiced
often, the movement will strengthen your heart and improve your blood
circulation.

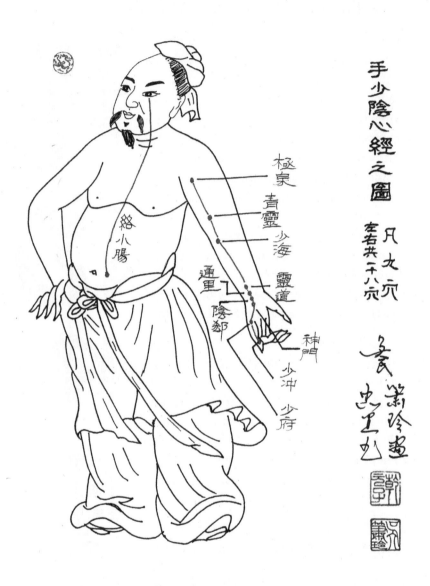

手少陰心經之圖　凡九穴　左右共十八穴

極泉
青靈　少海　靈道
通里
陰郄
神門
少衝　少府
絡小腸

V. Hand Shaoyin Heart Meridian

Heart Meridian

Movement: Deepen your horse stance. Circle your arms, bringing your right hand, palm facing up, to the level of the lower DanTian and raising your left hand, palm facing down, to the level of the middle DanTian. Keeping your two LaoGong in connection, open your arms wide, with your hands rotating the Qi ball between them. Then close your arms and bring your hands back to the previous position. Repeat this movement three times. As you open and close your arms, feel your entire body (especially the DanTian) open and close three times to symbolize the three layers of the universe and the three DanTian. When performing this movement, make sure that your LaoGong stay linked at all times, to hold the energy.

Visualization: Imagine you are embracing the sun and moon as you open and close your hands. The left hand is the sun and the right is the moon. This is Yin and Yang combining.

Breathing: Inhale as you open and exhale as you close, creating a big circle with your arms.

Function: This movement strengthens Heart and Lung functions and strengthens the Qi. It opens and sensitizes the LaoGong to both transmitting and receiving energy. It enables us to better understand and embody the Yin-Yang principle.

5.10 BaoYiShangShan 抱一上山
– Tiger Climbs the Mountain

Meaning: Bao means hold. **Yi** means oneness and also represents the Dao. Holding the oneness means living in the Dao. **Shang** means elevate, climb, and rise. **Shan** means mountain, which symbolizes Qi. Mountains are high and close to Heaven. They are sacred places where hermits engage in spiritual cultivation and connect and communicate with Heaven. The symbolic meaning of this movement is that we need to learn how to retreat from our busy lives.

JieQi 節氣: This movement is related to XiaZhi 夏至 (Summer Solstice). The tenth JieQi of a year, it is the midpoint of the Horse month (fifth month) and the middle summer month. It represents the zenith of life. Practicing this movement of the Tiger form will help you resonate with this seasonal energy and will help you find your utmost wisdom and inner power.

JingMai 經脈 (Meridians and Channels): Of the twelve organ meridians, this movement is connected with the ShouShaoYinXinJing 手少陰心經 (Hand Less Yin Heart Meridian, see Section 5.9). Of the eight extraordinary channels, the movement is interrelated with DuMai 督脈 (Governing Channel). This indicates that when practiced often, the movement will strengthen the functioning of your heart, kidney, and brain.

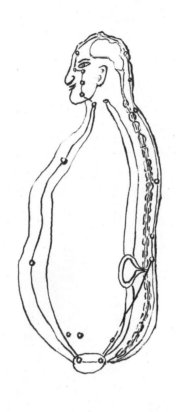

Governing Channel

Movement: Pivot back to the right with left palm (LaoGong, PC 8) connected to the inside of the elbow (ShaoHai 少海, HT 3). Snap your hands forward and form tiger claws with your fingers. The right hand is at about chest level and the left hand is at the level of the lower DanTian. Move your hands up and down, with the whole body moving in a climbing motion. Again, the energy must be held with the fingers as though they are claws. Pump the Qi in the arm and leg meridians.

Visualization: Visualize yourself as the tiger climbing up the mountain. Feel your whole body moving and all the parts cooperating with each other, especially the four limbs and claws. The tiger body is heavy, yet swift, sinuous, and agile. This illustrates Yin and Yang – lightness and heaviness contained in one being. The heaviness is in the bones – condensed and never yielding. The lightness is in the agility of the movement. The tiger is stable and rooted, while at the same time agile and active.

Breathing: Inhale deeply, gathering Qi into your lower DanTian. Breathe out and make the sound of the tiger growling and roaring.

Function: This movement strengthens the life force, the tendons, and the self-healing power, all of which are related to the eastern direction. Physically, it opens all the meridians and joints to allow for the free flow of Qi. It is especially good for joint problems and kidney disease.

5.11 YuFengXiaShan 御風下山 – Ride the Wind Down the Mountain

Meaning: Yu means ride, control. **Feng** means wind. The wind, or air, corresponds to Qi; as Confucius says, "FengCongHu 風從虎" (the wind follows the tiger).[1] Where there is wind, there is tiger energy. Wind is a reference to the breath of nature, as well as to the naturalness and unrestrained manner of the tiger. Like the wind, tiger comes and goes as it pleases, showing up suddenly and unexpectedly – sometimes with devastating force. According to the *HuangDiNeiJing*, as a pathological influence, wind is "the principal of all diseases," just as the tiger is often regarded as the principal of all vicious predators. **Xia** means descend, lower, down. **Shan** means mountain. **XiaShan** symbolizes the return of the enlightened hermit to civilization. **YuFeng** literally means riding the wind – in other words, learning how to control the energy and live in a harmonious state. **YuFeng** also symbolizes flying. Ancient shamanic stories tell us that the tiger is a bridge for human beings to reach Heaven. The symbolic meaning of this movement is that a hermit, having attained Enlightenment, descends back down to the mundane world to assist the rest of humanity. After his/her stay on the mountain, he/she has achieved the capability to "fly," and it is now time for the hermit to remember his/her humanity and help others. In our own cultivation, we need to remember this aspect of being human. In the energetic layers of the body, when you build up stronger Qi through your practice, Qi will "come down" to help weak parts of the body. This movement is also connected with Hexagram 11 – Tai 泰, the way of balance and stability.

1　Confucius, *XiCi*, one of the Ten Wings of *Yijing*.

JieQi 節氣: This movement is related to XiaoShu 小暑 (Minor Heat). The eleventh JieQi of a year, it is the starting point of the Goat month (sixth month) and the last summer month. It represents humanity and sharing your talent with others. Practicing this movement of the Tiger form will help you resonate with this seasonal energy and will help you cultivate great compassion.

JingMai 經脈 (Meridians and Channels): Of the twelve organ meridians, this movement is connected with the ShouTaiYangXiaoChangJing 手太陽小腸經 (Hand Great Yang Small Intestine Meridian). Of the eight extraordinary channels, the movement is associated with DuMai 督脈 (Governing Channel, see Section 5.10). This indicates that when practiced often, the movement will strengthen the functioning of your small intestine, kidney, and brain.

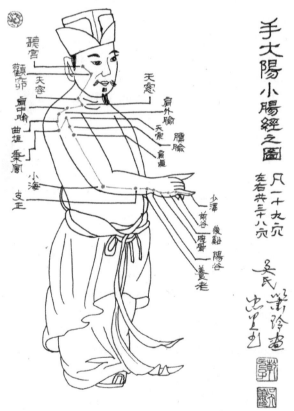

VI. Hand Taiyang Small Intestine Meridian

Small Intestine Meridian

Movement: Pivot to the left. Your left hand stays at the level of the DanTian, while your right hand floats up to gently stir Heaven and gather the Qi. Pivot your left heel slightly to the left to allow the right knee enough room to end up in the space just to the left of it. Curl your right wrist downward so that your fingers are pointing into the right shoulder (JianJing 肩井, GB 21), with the back of your hand pointing toward your right ear. In one swift motion, jab your right hand down in front of your right shoulder towards your left foot (YongChuan 湧泉, KD 1), bring your left hand up in front of your right cheek, and drop into a deep crouching position with your right knee just to the left of your left heel. Both palms should be facing to the right, claws extended to ward off enemies. As your balance in this position improves, pump up and down with your legs to work the meridians.

Visualization: When starting to transition from climbing the mountain, you stir the wind with your hands. During this movement, feel as if you are riding on and gathering the wind. Visualize feeling very light, as if your body has merged with the Qi. It is important to remember also to feel stable and grounded like the tiger. Hold the Qi, the wind, for a moment and then descend suddenly and smoothly – there is no blockage between the upper and the lower.

Breathing: Inhale, then exhale with Heng when descending.

Function: This movement will help to strengthen Kidney energy, and from a martial arts perspective, it is one of the best attack-and-defense positions. As wind carries the power of transformation, this movement is a way to release stagnation of the physical or spiritual bodies. The movement also benefits the twelve joints: shoulders, elbows, wrists, hips, knees, and ankles. It is a good way to open your spiritual gates and let the energy flow.

5.12 QiGuanChangHong 气贯長虹 – Qi Transforms into a Rainbow

Meaning: Qi has the same meaning as the Qi (Vital energy) in Qigong. **Guan** means link, penetrate. **Chang** means long, everlasting. **Hong** means rainbow. In Chinese shamanism, the rainbow is a symbol for dragon and it is also a bridge linking Heaven and Earth. This movement symbolizes strong Qi that is capable of creating a union between the human being and nature. The symbolic meaning of this movement is the tiger transforming into the dragon – a marked change in form and function. It also represents the communication between east and west and the harmony of Yin and Yang.

JieQi 節氣: This movement is related to DaShu 大暑 (Major Heat). The twelfth JieQi of a year, it is the midpoint of the Goat month (sixth month) and the last summer month. It represents great spiritual transformation. Practicing this movement of the Tiger form will help you resonate with this seasonal energy and will awaken your deepest levels of consciousness.

JingMai 經脈 **(Meridians and Channels):** Of the twelve organs meridians, this movement is connected with the ShouTaiYangXiaoChangJing 手太陽小腸經 (Hand Great Yang Small Intestine Meridian, see Section 5.11). Of the eight extraordinary channels, the movement is associated with DuMai 督脈 (Governing Channel, see Section 5.10). As with the previous movement, this indicates that when practiced often, this movement will strengthen the functioning of your small intestine, kidney, and brain.

Movement: Prepare to rise; allow your left hand, which is up by your right cheek, to descend with palm forward. Draw a big arc with your hands and arms, at the same time twisting your body at the waist to come back to center. Palms are forward and up, eventually turning palms up with fingers pointing towards each other over your head. In this movement, only the left wrist turns.

Visualization: As the hands are raised, imagine them full of Qi as the rainbow rises from earth to heaven.

Breathing: Take a deep breath at the start and exhale as you raise your hands and body.

Function: This movement stretches and opens the meridians and lets the Qi flow. It also stretches the tendons and benefits liver function.

Autumn Tiger

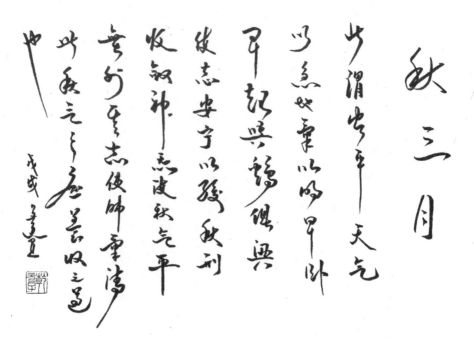

Autumn Quotation Calligraphy by Master Zhongxian Wu

秋三月，此謂容平，天氣以急，地氣以明，早臥早起，與雞俱興，使志安寧，以緩秋刑，收斂神氣，使秋氣平，無外其志，使肺氣清，此秋氣之應，養收之道也。

QiuSanYue, CiWeiRongPing, TianQiYiJi, DiQiYiMing, ZaoWoZaoQi, YuJiJuXing, ShiZhiAnNing, YiHuanQiuXing, ShouLianShenQi, ShiQiuQiPing, WuWaiQiZhi, ShiFeiQiQing, CiQiuQiZhiYing, YangShouZhiDaoYe.

The three months of autumn season are called RongPing 容平, which means to hold the peace. In this season, Heavenly Qi is sharp and Earthly Qi bright. You should go to bed early and get up early, and do your cultivation when the morning rooster crows – this will calm your mind and soften your interaction with the sharp autumn energy. Withdrawing your spiritual energy will make your autumn peaceful. Having no external ambitions will clear your Lungs. Above all, resonate with the autumn Qi, the Dao of gathering your life energy.

5.13 YunXingYuShi 雲行雨施
– Moving Clouds Make Rain

Meaning: Yun means clouds. **Xing** means move, do, element, achieve. **Yu** means rain. **Shi** means give, execute. The Chinese concept of clouds and rain contains sexual connotations: clouds and rain, a Chinese traditional synonym for intercourse, is the way of giving birth to new life. In traditional Chinese literature, intercourse is likened to clouds – clouds are the Qi that is produced when heaven and earth embrace, while ejaculation is equivalent to the bursting of the clouds, bringing forth fertilizing rain. Tigers are known to vocalize most vigorously when mating or fighting over a mate. As Yang creatures, tigers exhibit sexual prowess and their body parts are treasured aphrodisiacs. Tigers have frequent intercourse, climaxing in a dramatic ejaculation when the male tiger roars and bites his partner's neck.

This movement is the intercourse of Yin and Yang – a pattern of harmony. The combination of Yin and Yang is an expression of the Dao. Qigong practice is about harmonizing the Yin and the Yang, which will help maintain one's health and vital energy. With the appropriate amount of rain, the earth will give birth to all things. The pattern of this form is like the clouds making rain.

JieQi 節氣: This movement is related to LiQiu 立秋 (Autumn begins). The thirteenth JieQi of a year, it is the starting point of the Monkey month (seventh month) and the first autumn month. It represents changing the character of life. Practicing this movement of the Tiger form will help you resonate with this seasonal energy and will help you break old life patterns that no longer serve you and re-establish your new sense of balance.

JingMai 經脈 **(Meridians and Channels):** Of the twelve organs meridians, this movement is connected with the ZuTaiYangPangGuangJing 足太陽膀胱經 (Foot Great Yang Bladder Meridian). Of the eight extraordinary channels, the movement is associated with YinQiaoMai 陰蹻脈 (Yin Bridge Channel). This indicates that when practiced often, the movement will strengthen the functioning of your bladder, kidney, and heart.

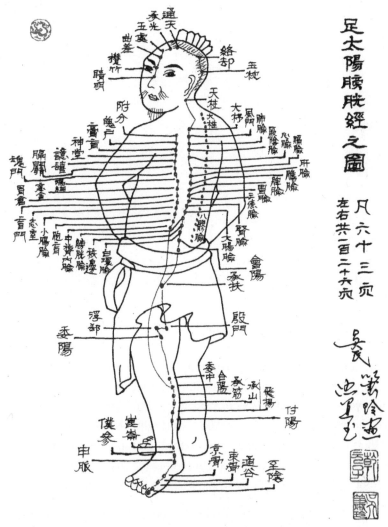

VII. Foot Taiyang Bladder Meridian

Bladder Meridian

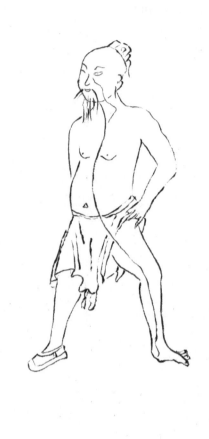

Yin Bridge Channel

Movement: Allow your arms to descend with fingers pointed up, relaxing the fingers so they become horizontal at about shoulder level. As you lower your arms to the level of your lower DanTian, lower your body to come back into horse stance. You are bringing the heavenly energy to earth and connecting heaven and earth. It is important not to loosen your arms as they move down; you must hold the energy. Keep your head upright and your upper body straight during the movement.

Visualization: Imagine clouds in the sky above. The clouds become rain that falls down to earth and invigorates the body.

Breathing: Breathe in while you hold your hands at the top for a moment; then exhale, and relax as your hands move down.

Function: This is a soft Yin movement that nourishes the body. Yin nourishes Yang. This movement is good for Yin deficiency or Kidney Yin deficiency. It is a way to strengthen your sexual power. It is also good for excess Yang conditions, such as insomnia and hypertension. Blood pressure can be reduced even by simply visualizing the falling rain, although the movement along with the visualization is, of course, more effective (to achieve long-term stabilization of your blood pressure, please do this movement daily).

5.14 ErLongXiZhu 二龍戲珠 – Double Dragons Play with the Pearl

Meaning: Er means two, double. **Long** means dragon. **Xi** means to play, perform. **Zhu** means pearl, treasure. From a Chinese shamanic perspective, the pearl represents the storage of all the dragon's power and magic. If the dragon loses its pearl, it will lose all its power and will be unable to make rain or transformations. Since the days of ancient Chinese shamanism, the pearl has represented the finest energy or elixir in internal alchemy practices. Refining the pearl or the elixir of our body via Qigong cultivation is augmenting the life force – Jing, Qi, and Shen.

The dragon holds the pearl under its chin. In Qigong practice, the tongue should always be holding the upper palate; it is symbolic of holding the pearl. This is one of the most important techniques in making the elixir (in internal alchemy) – this harmonization of Yin and Yang internally is what produces the elixir. Double Dragons Play with the Pearl is fundamentally playing with the Qi.

JieQi 節氣: This movement is related to ChuShu 處暑 (Heat settles down). The fourteenth JieQi of a year, it is the midpoint of the Monkey month (seventh month) and the first autumn month. It represents the joyful nature of life. Practicing this movement of the Tiger form will help you resonate with this seasonal energy and will settle you down and help you to rediscover the joy of life.

JingMai 經脈 (Meridians and Channels): Of the twelve organs meridians, this movement is connected with the ZuTaiYangPangGuangJing 足太陽膀胱經 (Foot Great Yang Bladder Meridian, see Section 5.13).

Of the eight extraordinary channels, the movement is associated with YinQiaoMai 陰蹻脈 (Yin Bridge Channel, see Section 5.13). As with the previous movement, this indicates that when practiced often, this movement will strengthen the functioning of your bladder, kidney, and heart.

Movement: Rotate your wrists and turn your palms up. Extend your arms behind you. Rotate your wrists again to come forward with your LaoGong facing heaven. This is a spiral motion and you will raise your hands above your head, fingers pointing to each other, palm up. Both arms are like a double dragon spiraling and raising the pearl toward heaven. Remember, palms should always be facing up during this movement, as you repeat it again and again.

Visualization: Visualize your hands holding the Pearl/Qi ball to refine your external Qi and healing capabilities. Visualize the two arms as two flying dragons playing with the Pearl/Qi ball.

Breathing: Start taking a deep breath when your arms are at the lowest point, then continue inhaling and raise your arms up toward heaven. Keep inhaling until the arms reach as far as they can over the head. Exhale on the way down.

Function: This movement helps open the meridians and refines the Qi. It is great way to strengthen your external Qi and healing power. It is especially good for the shoulders, arms, and Triple Burner. It also opens the spine and benefits all the problems related to the spine.

5.15 TiHuGuanDing 醍醐灌頂
– Heavenly Dew Purifies the Body

Meaning: TiHu refers to refined milk, a substance that is powerfully nutritious. For the purpose of our practice, the nutrition referred to here is spiritual nourishment. **Guan** means to pour. **Ding** refers to the top of your head. This movement is a way to open the gate of wisdom, symbolizing not only the way of physical wellness resulting from Qigong, but also the way of spiritual enlightenment. It also means the pleasure of receiving wisdom, like pouring rich liqueur over one's head.

JieQi 節氣: This movement is related to BaiLu 白露 (White Dew). The fifteenth JieQi of a year, it is the starting point of the Rooster month (eighth month) and the middle autumn month. It represents the clarity of brain. Practicing this movement of the Tiger form will help you resonate with this seasonal energy and will sharpen your mind.

JingMai 經脈 (Meridians and Channels):
Of the twelve organ meridians, this movement is connected with the ZuShaoYinShenJing 足少陰腎經 (Foot Less Yin Kidney Meridian). Of the eight extraordinary channels, the movement is associated with YinQiaoMai 陰蹻脈 (Yin Bridge Channel, see Section 5.13). This indicates that when practiced often, the movement will strengthen the functioning of your kidney and heart, and nourish your Shen.

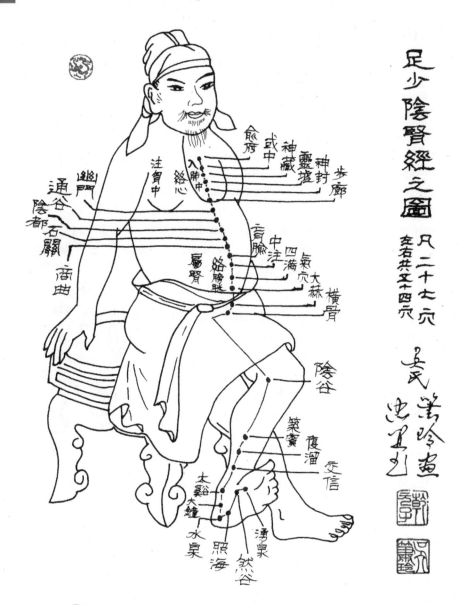

VIII. Foot Shaoyin Kidney Meridian

Kidney Meridian

Movement: Rotate your hands toward heaven to gather the universal Qi and then turn the palms down, facing your head. You can hold this posture for few minutes. Lower your hands – descending, purifying, and rooting into the earth with the Qi. End with your hands at the level of the lower DanTian.

Visualization: Imagine bringing the dew from heaven into your body and down to earth. This heavenly dew is pouring through the top of your head to nourish the body and spirit. It is an inner shower of purification.

Breathing: Inhale and rotate your hands over your head, then exhale as you turn your palms down to face the earth. Hold your posture and regulate your breathing to be slow, smooth, deep, and even. Make the Heng mantra as you bring your hands down.

Function: This movement purifies the physical body as well as the energetic heart. Its function is to move one into a deeper layer of meditation. During this movement, your consciousness will be resonating at a high level. One physical phenomenon of this state is that your saliva (heavenly dew) will be more refined, more abundant, and will produce a special calming smell. It will purify and nourish the body and Shen.

5.16 JinGuiXiaHai 金龜下海 – Golden Turtle Plunges into the Ocean

Meaning: Jin means metal, gold, golden color. **Gui** means turtle. Turtles can find their way back to the place where they were born, no matter how far away they have roamed. Turtles have the innate ability to navigate long routes in the ocean and to remember the origin of their journeys. Turtles are water animals but their shells are like armor, which symbolizes protective energy (Wei Qi) and thereby relates the turtle to the Metal element (Metal generates Water). Turtles have the ability to go for indeterminate amounts of time without food, taking Qi from the air. The Golden Turtle is a symbol for longevity, the northern direction, and the spiritual energy related to the prenatal energy of the kidney. **Xia** means plunge into, submerge, lower, reduce, descend. **Hai** means sea, ocean. Water is the prenatal root of life on Earth and of memory. This movement is a symbol for returning to the Dao. It is related to the shamanic way of understanding the cycles of life and death. It imitates a turtle and it is good for helping us remember who we are. It is a way to discover our universal lineage and roots.

JieQi 節氣: This movement is related to QiuFen 秋分 (Autumn Equinox). The sixteenth JieQi of a year, it is the midpoint of the Rooster month (eighth month) and the middle autumn month. It represents spiritual equilibrium and righteousness. Practicing this movement of the Tiger form will help you resonate with this seasonal energy and will strengthen your Lung function and sensitivity.

JingMai 經脈 (Meridians and Channels): Of the twelve organ meridians, this movement is connected with the ZuShaoYinShenJing 足少陰 腎經 (Foot Less Yin Kidney Meridian, see Section 5.15). Of the eight extraordinary channels, the movement is associated with DaiMai 帶脈 (Belt Channel). This indicates that when practiced often, the movement will strengthen your kidneys and YangQi.

Belt Channel

Movement: Take a deep breath and allow yourself to open, feeling your fingers touch the ends of the universe as you gather the universal Qi. Your toes are still grabbing the ground, your back is bent slightly forward from the waist, and all the muscles in your hips are tight. This position mimics the turtle swimming into the ocean. Rotate your fingers toward the MingMen 命門 and gather the Qi in your kidneys with the mantra of Hai Hei 嗨嘿 and with your LaoGong pointing at each kidney.

Visualization: Imagine yourself as a turtle plunging into the ocean, navigating underwater to find your way home. Gather the Qi and the essence of the ocean as your LaoGong point to your kidneys, storing the Qi and Essence within.

Breathing: Take a deep breath and inhale as you open your arms. Exhale as your fingers reach behind you with the Hai Hei mantra with your fingers pointing to your kidneys.

Function: This movement works with Shen energy to tonify (strengthen) the heart. It works to tonify the kidney and to dispel all diseases related to kidney, such as low back pain, knee pain, and leg pain. It is good for people who have poor memories. It is a way to learn about the importance of the treasure Jing (Essence) of the prenatal body, the Kidney Water in daily life, which is the root of our spiritual cultivation.

5.17 JingTaoHuiDang 錦濤回蕩 – Colorful Wave Cleanses the Spirit

Meaning: Jing means colorful, brocade. **Tao** means wave, tide. **Hui** means return. **Dang** means wash away, rush. This movement symbolizes purification, as in the ocean having the ability to purify the land. Here, we are returning again to the emotion and spiritual layers of the body to purify on a deeper layer. The golden color of the tide is produced from the shining sun. The reflecting water becomes a symbol for Shen or spirit. The colorful wave is a symbol for the harmonization of fire and water. Jing is related to Metal, combining the Yin element of Water with the Yang element of the sun.

The journey of internal cultivation is not easy and, in fact, may be quite difficult, so one needs to continue to practice in order to purify the physical body and spiritual body, washing away resistance and blockages. The practice is not just about the movement, but about your inner world. You use the mind to purify all stagnations, to wash away difficulties. The message becomes one of spiritual cultivation.

JieQi 節氣: This movement is related to HanLu 寒露 (Cold Dew). The seventeenth JieQi of a year, it is the turning point of the Dog month (ninth month), the last autumn month. It represents the spiritual purification of nature. Practicing this movement of the Tiger form will help you resonate with this seasonal energy and help you clear up stagnations and remove blockages from all aspects of your being.

JingMai 經脈 **(Meridians and Channels):** Of the twelve organ meridians, this movement is connected with the ShouJueYinXinBaoJing 手厥陰心包經 (Hand Sealed Yin Pericardium Meridian). Of the eight extraordinary channels, the movement is interrelated with DaiMai 帶脈 (Belt Channel, see Section 5.16). This indicates that when practiced often, the movement will strengthen your heart and YangQi.

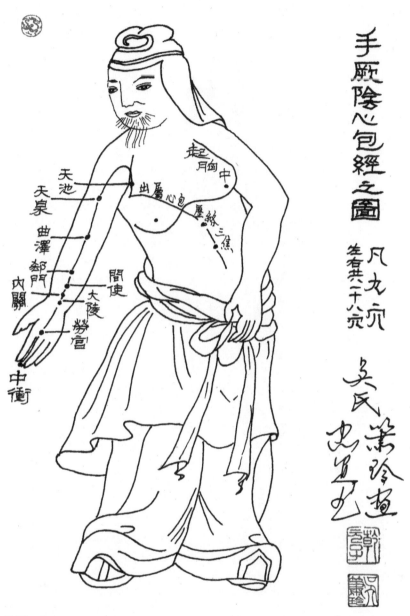

IX. Hand Jueyin Pericardium Meridian

Pericardium Meridian

Movement: Bring your arms forward. Raise your hands, with palm up, to chest level and facing your chest. Inhale and bring your arms toward you, then exhale and let them flow out away from you. Repeat this movement a few times. It should be smooth and peaceful, mimicking the motion of ocean waves.

Visualization: Imagine a colorful wave in the sunlight, washing and purifying your spirit. Feel the rhythmic motion of the tide as you merge yourself with this wave. Exhale and breathe out all negativity and toxins. Purify the deepest layers of the body.

Breathing: Inhale and bring your hands toward your body, then exhale as you turn your hands outward with the mantra Hu 呼 (form your lips in a small pucker and blow the air out while just barely audibly making the mantra).

Function: With this movement, we are washing the heart and lung, purifying our emotions. This movement promotes structural, functional, and energetic wellness of the heart and lung. It also tonifies the spleen and aids in the release of the emotions belonging to the heart, lung, and spleen, namely anxiety and sadness. It works to purify the mind and Shen in general.

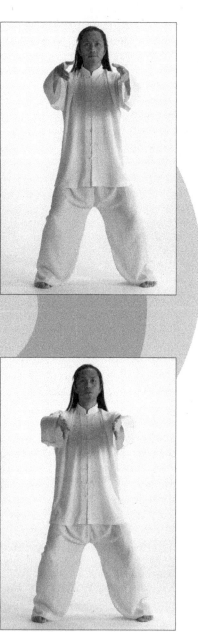

5.18 DanFengChaoYang 丹鳳朝陽 – Red Phoenix Visits the Sun

Meaning: Dan means red, which is the color of spirit, and also means elixir. **Feng** means phoenix, the symbol for the spirit. **Chao** means face but also means to meet someone in a higher position or from an older generation. Here, it means to raise your spiritual energy. **Yang** means the sun. The sun is a symbol of the Yang energy of the universe and also the spirit of the body. In this movement, the Red Phoenix is the spiritual animal of the south and is thus related to the heart. The Red Phoenix visiting the sun represents the pure Yang state of cultivation, which refers to the body transforming into a state of immortality or Enlightenment. Through practicing this movement, we learn to purify our bodies and work through the difficulties involved in moving toward the pure Yang state and understanding the processes therein.

JieQi 節氣: This movement is related to ShuangJiang 霜降 (Frost descends). The eighteenth JieQi of a year, it is the midpoint of the Dog month (ninth month), the last autumn month. It represents detachment and enlightenment. Practicing this movement of the Tiger form will help you resonate with this seasonal energy and will profoundly awaken your inner wisdom.

JingMai 經脈 (Meridians and Channels): Of the twelve organ meridians, this movement is connected with the ShouJueYinXinBaoJing 手厥陰心包經 (Hand Sealed Yin Pericardium Meridian, see Section 5.17). Of the eight extraordinary channels, the movement is interrelated with DaiMai 帶脈 (Belt Channel, see Section 5.16). This indicates that when practiced often, the movement will strengthen your heart and YangQi.

Movement: On the last exhale, breathe in again and bring your hands toward you. On your next exhale, snap your hands with palms forward and arms extended in front of you. Hold this circle as you raise your arms above your head and hold your posture.

Visualization: Imagine yourself as the Red Phoenix flying into Heaven and holding the Sun up with your hands.

Breathing: Take a deep breath as you raise your arms over your head and hold your breath as long as you can. Exhale as you bring your arms down. Be mindful of lifting your perineum to hold onto the energy during your exhale.

Function: Holding this posture will strengthen your Fire and Earth energy since Fire gives birth to Earth. This movement strengthens the physical function of the shoulders and heart and also strengthens the spiritual function of the Heart Shen/Spirit. It can also assist in curing diarrhea.

Winter Tiger

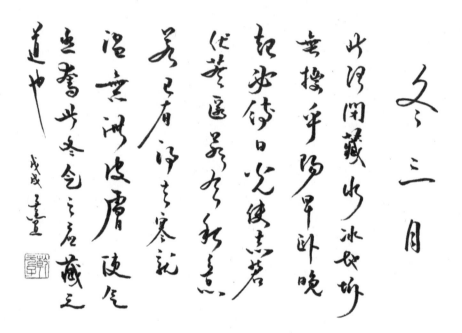

Winter Quotation Calligraphy by Master Zhongxian Wu

冬三月
此謂閉藏
水冰地坼
無擾乎陽
早臥晚起
必待日光
使志若伏若匿
若已有得
若有私意
去寒就溫
無泄皮膚
使氣亟奪
此冬氣之應
養藏之道也

DongSanYue, CiWeiBiCang, ShuiBingDiChe, WuRaoHuYang,
ZaoWoWanQi, BiDaiRiGuang, ShiZhiRuoFuRuoNi,
RuoYouSiYi, RuoYiYouDe, QuHanJiuWen, WuXiePiFu,
ShiQiJiDuo, CiDongQiZhiYing, YangCangZhiDaoYe.

The three months of winter season are called BiCang 閉藏, which means sealing the storage. During this season, water becomes ice and the land cracks; therefore, do not disturb your Yang energy. You should go to bed early and get up late, waiting until sunrise. Hold your spirit deep within, as if you are guarding your privacy or hiding a secret treasure. Avoid the cold and keep warm. Do not make excess sweat on your skin; otherwise you will quickly leak your Qi. Above all, resonate with the winter Qi, the Dao of storing your life energy.

5.19 ShuiZhongLaoYue 水中撈月 – Lift the Moon from the Water

Meaning: Shui means water. **Zhong** means center, within, inside. **Lao** means pick up, lift. **Yue** means moon. The image of the moon in the water is a symbol for emptiness, of the material world and the emptiness within it. The moon in the water is only a reflection of the physical moon that exists. Qigong practice can help us deeply understand this emptiness. Everything in existence has some degree of relationship, some level of connection – if you see the moon in water, there will also be a moon in the sky. The reflection shows both emptiness and actual existence. Real emptiness is not empty because there is actually something there. Just like the reflection of the moon in the water, you would not be able to physically pick up this moon; the reflection reminds us that the moon is in the sky right at the exact moment. Also, you would never see the real moon, up in the heavens, if you only focus on the moon's reflection. In order to see the real moon, you will have to detach from your yearning for the moon in the water and turn your head toward the sky. This analogy allows us to understand the principle of Emptiness in our cultivation practice. Once we dedicate ourselves to the Dao, we learn emptiness and the need to break our attachments to the material world. In a certain way, the material world can be a distraction, just like the moon in the water, which can bring some level of resistance to our practice.

JieQi 節氣: This movement is related to LiDong 立冬 (Winter begins). The nineteenth JieQi of a year, it is the turning point of the winter season and the Pig month (tenth month), the first winter month. It represents the time to preserve your life energy. Practicing this movement of the Tiger form will help you resonate with this seasonal energy and will help you restore your life source.

JingMai 經脈 (Meridians and Channels): Of the twelve organ meridians, this movement is connected with the ShouShaoYangSanJiaoJing 手少陽三焦經 (Hand Less Yang Triple Burner Meridian). Of the eight extraordinary channels, the movement is interrelated with YangWeiMai 陽維脈 (Yang Safeguard Channel). This indicates that when practiced often, the movement will strengthen your immune system.

Movement: Inhale again, then exhale and begin to lower with your arms and come into a squat. Draw a circle with your arms and hands, descending all the way down to the earth while maintaining your posture with a straight back and neck. Keep the upper body straight, regardless of how low you can go. When your arms and hands complete the circle, reach down to scoop up the moon from the bottom of the ocean. It is important to maintain the lift in your perineum and not let energy leak as you descend.

Visualization: Imagine pulling or lifting the moon out of the ocean.

Breathing: Lift your hands as you inhale deeply. Then hold your breath as long as you can. Remember to lift your perineum.

Function: This movement benefits the kidneys and helps with knee and leg problems. It brings us closer to the way of Enlightenment. It allows us to open to the wisdom we already hold, enabling us to grasp emptiness.

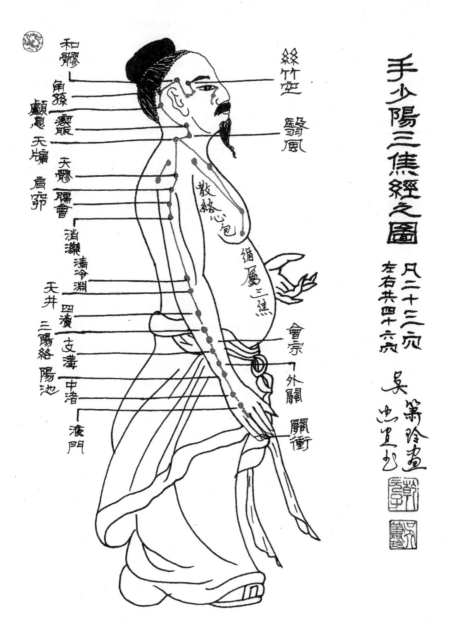

X. Hand Shaoyang Triple Burner Meridian

Triple Burner Meridian

陽維脈循行圖

Yang Safeguard Channel

5.20 LongTengHuYue 龍騰虎躍 – Dragon and Tiger Leap into Heaven

Meaning: Long means dragon. **Teng** means jumping, leaping. **Hu** means tiger. **Yue** means jump from one place to another, like jumping over a stream. **Yue** also means going to heaven to connect with high-level beings. The leaping in this movement symbolizes two substances, Qi and Jing, which transform into Shen and bring us closer to the Dao. This movement symbolizes east and west cooperating in Yin-Yang balance. In shamanism, the dragon and tiger are symbols for elevation. The dragon of the east represents YuanJing 元精 or original essence in the body, while the tiger of the west represents YuanQi 元气 or original Qi. These two substances combine and transform in the body to nourish Shen or spirit.

JieQi 節氣: This movement is related to XiaoXue 小雪 (Minor Snow). The twentieth JieQi of a year, it is the midpoint of the Pig month (tenth month), the first winter month. It represents the time to maintain the inner Fire. Practicing this movement of the Tiger form will help you resonate with this seasonal energy and will help you boost the fire in your life Fire and cultivate your free-flowing Qi.

JingMai 經脈 (Meridians and Channels): Of the twelve organs meridians, this movement is connected with the ShouShaoYangSanJiaoJing 手少陽三焦經 (Hand Less Yang Triple Burner Meridian, see Section 5.19). Of the eight extraordinary channels, the movement is interrelated with YangWeiMai 陽維脈 (Yang Safeguard Channel, see Section 5.19). As with the previous movement, this indicates that when practiced often, the movement will strengthen your immune system.

Movement: Pick up the moon and begin raising only your arms, still lifting your perineum and holding your posture. When your hands are at the level of your ears, rotate them with palms facing away from you and fingers pointing toward heaven. Quickly jump up into heaven and feel your fingers touching heaven. Move your hips, your whole body, as you stretch upward.

Visualization: The left arm represents the dragon and the right arm represents the tiger. As these animals rise and leap into heaven, feel your own fingers touching heaven. Feel your whole body expanding.

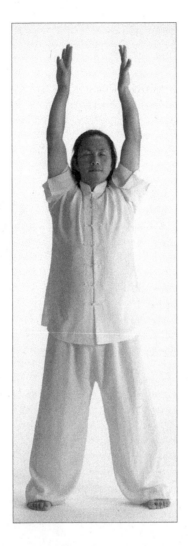

Breathing: Hold your breath, and with a quick breath out, leap as you straighten your body. Your breath should be evenly regulated as you stretch.

Function: This movement harmonizes the Yin-Yang energy. In the physical layer, it works to release any kind of disease. This movement transforms energy by opening the spiritual gates of the body and harmonizing the Yin-Yang Qi to purify the body. This allows for smooth energy flow and a unification of Yin and Yang. It is a way to refine the body's energy.

5.21 HuiFengHunHe 迴风混合 – Harmonizing Wind Unites the Cosmos

Meaning: Hui means whirlpool and also means return. **Feng** means wind. In shamanism, **Feng** represents the circulation of Qi. **Hun** means blend, mix, merge. **He** means combine, unite, union, harmony, peace.

In Qigong practice, one should always bring energy together in the "cauldron," which is located in the lower belly, to be refined. One needs to control the wind very well to refine the energy. In Daoist internal alchemy, refining the elixir is a path to allow the mind, breath, and body to unite together in the last step to becoming symbolically immortal. After Jing, Qi, and Shen are harmonized and further sophisticated, one will be enlightened and resonate with the Dao.

JieQi 節氣: This movement is related to DaXue 大雪 (Major Snow). The twenty-first JieQi of a year, it is the initial point of the Rat month (eleventh month), the middle winter month. It represents the time to turn your attention deep within to preserve your life source. Practicing this movement of the Tiger form will help you resonate with this seasonal energy and will help you find inner peace and harmony.

JingMai 經脈 (Meridians and Channels): Of the twelve organ meridians, this movement is associated with the ZuShaoYangDanJing 足少陽膽經 (Foot Less Yang Gallbladder Meridian). Of the eight extraordinary channels, the movement is connected with YangWeiMai 陽維脈 (Yang Safeguard Channel, see Section 5.19). This indicates that when practiced often, the movement will strengthen your immune system and the function of your gallbladder.

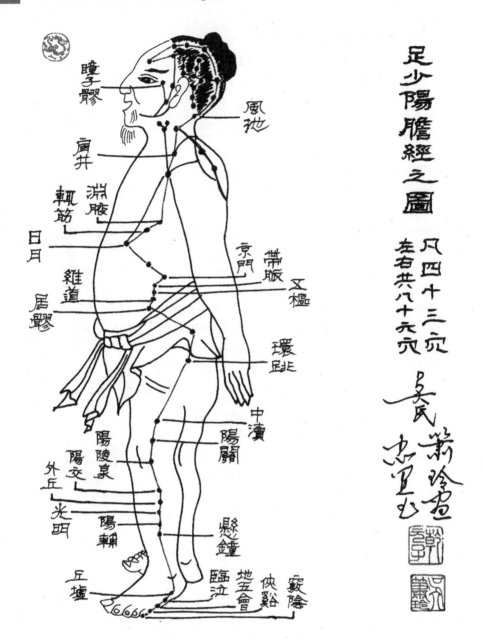

XI. Foot Shaoyang Gallbladder Meridian

Gallbladder Meridian

Movement: Rotate your fingers and wrists, holding the energy. Point your fingers toward earth, bringing them to the level of your ears with palms facing outward. Quickly lower your arms and legs with the Heng mantra. Focus on your wrists and bring them down in a snapping motion with fingers pointing toward the waist. Remember your posture: head is upright, knees are bent in horse stance, and toes are grabbing the earth.

Visualization: Visualize all the light of the Qi condensing in your lower DanTian. Visualize and feel the DanTian as the center of the universe.

Breathing: The breath should be regulated to a softened state, and you should feel that each breath is related to the lower DanTian. Once you have moved into this state, the breath will regulate itself naturally without conscious effort, as you merge with the light and Qi in your lower DanTian.

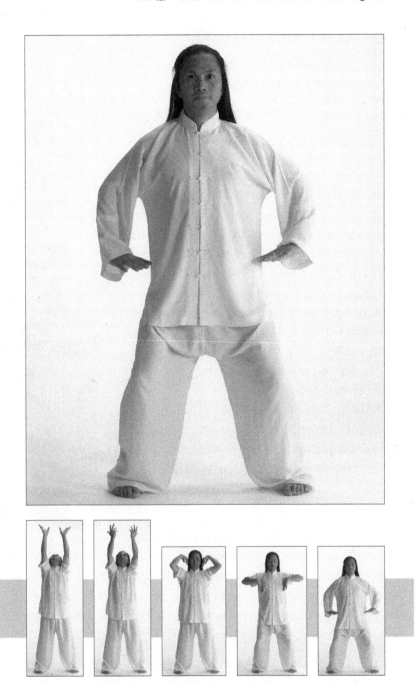

Function: This movement enables us to move into a harmonizing Qi state so we can understand the Dao.

5.22 WeiLingBaFang 威靈八方 – Maintain Peace in the Eight Directions

Meaning: **Wei** means dignity, power, impressive presence. **Ling** is usually translated as soul, spirit, shaman. **Ba** means eight and represents stableness and accomplishment. **Fang** means direction, way, and it stands for the cosmos. **BaFang** means eight directions, which includes all directions, and symbolizes the entire universe. One may start Qigong practice with a small personal request, such as to improve your state of health, to release life trauma, or to create power to heal. After a certain length of Qigong practice, one will be aware that Qigong is a method of helping people live in a natural state. We learn how to reach this state by serving others rather than by trying to fulfill personal desires.

This movement represents bringing the benefits of immortality to the universe, not just to one's personal world. It helps to deepen one's power of compassion and heartfelt desire to dedicate the practice and energy generated towards the benefit of others and Mother Nature.

JieQi 節氣: This movement is related to DongZhi 冬至 (Winter Solstice). The twenty-second JieQi of a year, it is the midpoint of the Rat month (eleventh month), the middle winter month. It represents the rebirth of new-life energy. Practicing this movement of the Tiger form will help you resonate with this seasonal energy and will help you remain in good health and prosperity.

JingMai 經脈 **(Meridians and Channels):** Of the twelve organs meridians, this movement is aligned with the ZuShaoYangDanJing 足少陽膽經 (Foot Less Yang Gallbladder Meridian, see Section 5.21). Of the eight extraordinary channels, the movement is connected with RenMai 任脈 (Conception Channel). This indicates that when practiced often, the movement will strengthen your immune system and the functioning of all your organs.

任脈循行圖

戊戌吴氏

蕭陰居

忠正书

Conception Channel

Movement: Maintain your body position in horse stance with your fingers pointing towards your waist as you move from side to side. Turn your head left as you shift to your left foot. Turn your head right as you shift to the right foot. Shift left and right a few times.

Visualization: Visualize driving off all evil energy, instilling and maintaining peace over the entire world.

Breathing: Exhale to either side as you imitate the roar of the tiger. Inhale when you switch sides and your head comes back to center.

Function: This movement strengthens the physical function of the whole body. It also generates healing power, especially the energy of deep compassion.

Eight Trigrams and Eight Directions of the Prenatal Taiji
BaGua 太極八卦 *Diagram, by Master Zhongxian Wu*

5.23 ChaoLiDongTian 朝禮洞天 – Sacrifice Everything to the Heavenly Cave

Meaning: Chao means face, moving from a lower position to an upper position. **Li** means sacrifice, ritual, celebration, humble. **Dong** means cave. **Tian** means Heaven, the universe. The connection here is that human beings originated in a cave – a womb. In the Chinese shamanic tradition, a cave is a sacred place in the body where one's primordial spirit (YuanShen 元神) dwells. The cave is also related to the tiger – remember I told you that the Queen Mother of the West lives in a cave, KunLunXu 崑崙虛, which is covered with tiger skin? **DongTian** literally means heavenly cave, and it is the symbol of a special sacred place. Heavenly cave represents the mystery of the Dao. This movement embodies the concept that the human being is not separate from the universe. We each have a spiritual body with its universal root. In Chinese, there is a saying: "SheDe 舍得 (To give is the way to gain)." In high-level Qigong cultivation, emptying your heart and sacrificing yourself to the Dao is an important process. This is the secret of an enlightened being's ability to achieve immortality. To clarify the Daoist concept of immortality, I would like to cite a little excerpt from an article I wrote several years ago:

> The idea of immortality or everlasting life has nothing to do with yearning to live forever. On a superficial level, of course no living being can escape death. Death is simply a part of the universal Five Elements natural cycle. However, death is always accompanied by the process of rebirth. In this way, there is no death. In the Immortal's tradition, we have an expression – XinSi ShenHuo 心死神活, which translates into English as "allow your heart to die so that your spirit

will live." By embracing death and bringing it gracefully into our hearts during practicing this posture, we will understand the knowledge of immortality.[2]

JieQi 節氣: This movement is related to XiaoHan 小寒 (Minor Cold). The twenty-third JieQi of a year, it is the beginning point of the Ox month (twelfth month), the last winter month. It represents the power of nature. Practicing this movement of the Tiger form will help you resonate with this seasonal energy and will help you find your supreme inner power, which will allow you to face and transform any challenges or traumas in your life.

JingMai 經脈 (Meridians and Channels): Of the twelve organ meridians, this movement is associated with the ZuJueYinGanJing 足厥陰肝經 (Foot Sealed Yin Liver Meridian). Of the eight extraordinary channels, the movement is tied with RenMai 任脈 (Conception Channel, see Section 5.22). This indicates that when practiced often, the movement will strengthen your life force and the functioning of all of your organs.

Movement: Stabilize your horse stance. Rotate your hands backward with palms up to extend behind you. Make a big circle with your arms coming forward to rest in the Taiji mudra at the level of the middle DanTian. Males will place the left hand under the right, while females will place right hand under the left. Your palms face earth. Bring your feet together with your knees slightly bent, holding a prayerful attitude.

---

2   Zhongxian Wu, "Energy Medicine and the Purpose of Cultivation – An interview with Jessica Kingsley, of Jessica Kingsley Publishers," *Singing Dragon Newsletter*, January 2012.

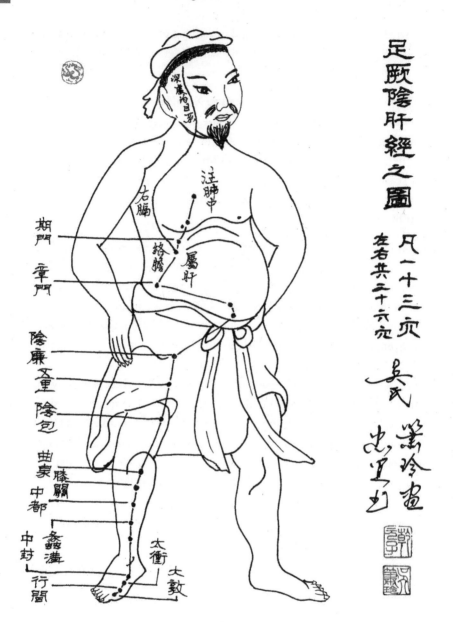

XII. Foot Jueyin Liver Meridian

Liver Meridian

Visualization: Imagine gathering the universal Qi when your feet and hands come together. Empty the physical body and the Heart-Mind. Dedicate the entirety of your being (mental, spiritual, and physical) to the Dao. You are returning to your cave.

Breathing: The breath is regulated from the lower DanTian. You can also perform holding-the-breath practice during this movement to further concentrate the energy in the lower DanTian and empty the heart.

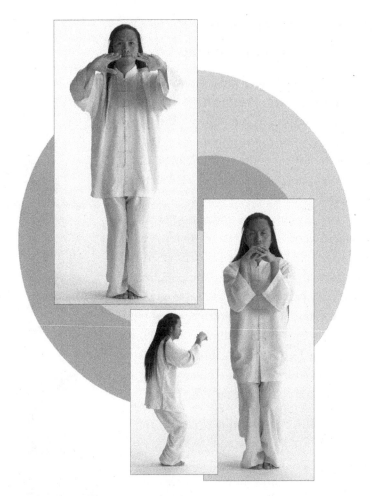

Function: This movement functions to release the ego and desire, which is a pathway to access one's original nature. This movement may release any disease for self-healing. It is an especially good way to enhance the energy of the heart and spirit. In Chinese medicine, we say that BingYouXinQi 病由心起 – all disease is related to the heart. As the heart is sacrificed, the body will return to a natural state. In relation to this sacrifice, in the shamanic tradition, one always gives the best to heaven. Again, when there is no giving, there is no gaining. LaoZi talked about this attitude of cultivation as "WaiQiShenErShenCun 外其身而身存 – The Mind remains outside of the body, but the body is always there." [3] This tells us that when we remove the concerns of the body from our mind, our body will take care of itself.

---

3   Laozi, *DaoDeJing*, Chapter 7.

5.24 DaoQiChangCun 道炁常存 – Remain in the Dao Qi

Meaning: Dao means road, the Way, and universal law. As for the Great Dao itself, words cannot be used to interpret it, but you can experience it through your inner cultivation. **Qi** is the vital breath of the Dao, the universal life force. **Chang** means eternal, always, continue, often. **Cun** means exist, be real, live.

The Dao is omnipotent and omnipresent. It is everywhere all of the time. Through our practice, we can access the Dao anytime and anywhere. The Dao is not only for those who are enlightened, extraordinary beings; it is very close to all human beings. Everyone has the ability to be enlightened. The difference is that the illuminated being is living with the Dao, staying on the Path in his/her deepest consciousness, and regular people may forget the Dao and thus live far away from it.

JieQi 節氣: This movement is related to DaHan 大寒 (Major Cold). The twenty-fourth JieQi of a year, it is the midpoint of the Ox month (twelfth month), the last winter month. It represents the challenging nature of life and spiritual cultivation. Practicing this movement of the Tiger form will help you resonate with this seasonal energy and will help you find the simple way to continue your daily cultivation and live with the Dao.

JingMai 經脈 **(Meridians and Channels):** Of the twelve organ meridians, this movement is associated with the ZuJueYinGanJing 足厥陰肝經 (Foot Sealed Yin Liver Meridian, see Section 5.23). Of the eight extraordinary channels, the movement is tied with RenMai 任脈 (Conception Channel, see Section 5.22). This indicates that when practiced often, the movement will strengthen your life force and the functioning of all of your organs.

Movement: Lower your arms and the Taiji mudra to return to the position of the very first movement. Make sure your posture is correct. Connect your LaoGong with your lower DanTian. Be in the Qi field. Be in the Dao. Observe your inner landscape.

Visualization: Visualize being back in your cave. Imagine your whole being merging with the light of the Dao.

Breathing: Regulate your breath from the lower DanTian. Soften your breath to a slow, smooth, deep, and even state.

Function: This movement maintains physical well-being and awakens within us the eternal Dao, which is always present. Actually, although this movement looks like doing nothing, it is an important part of Qigong practice. After all active movements, we need to move into the state of tranquility in order to cultivate our inner knowledge. This is a way to experience the Dao. This is the essence of Qigong, passed on by ancient Chinese shamans, to help people learn the eternal Dao. As LaoZi states in his *DaoDeJing*: ShengRenChuWuWeiZhiShi XingBuYanZhiJiao 聖人處無為之事 行不言之教 – "The sages (shamans) conduct their business with actionless actions and give their teachings with wordless words."[4]

---

4   Laozi, *DaoDeJing*, Chapter 2.

Afterword

Guan 觀 – Observe

Observe your inner balance and source of your life

萬物並作
吾以觀其復

WanWuBingZuo WuYiGuanQiFu

Ten-thousand-things are acting, I observe their return

LaoZi, *DaoDeJing* 道德經 (Chapter 16)

During this summer vacation season, I took some time off from my teachings and had the opportunity to write this book in my favorite, peaceful retreat-like setting on a small island in Stockholm's archipelago. I've done much writing at "Phoenix Nest" over the years. About two weeks ago, as the summer season ended (according to classical Chinese cosmology, this summer ended on August 7, 2018), I finished the main text. I found my inspiration for writing waning as the summer season drew to an end. I did not have any vision about how to conclude this book. I decided to let it go and instead took the time to simply enjoy my life and the natural world around me.

Then a strange thing happened! Well, perhaps you may not think it too strange if you are used to carefully observing the patterns of nature...

In the past two weeks, the earth has suddenly turned back to a lush green color, after several months of a very unusual scorching and drought-fraught summer. Everything had turned dry, brittle, brown, and yellowed, long before the autumn season began. However, with the turn of the season, the Autumn Tiger energy has brought fresh, spring-like energy to the natural world, instead of the "killing-Qi" we would expect.

Although abnormal fluctuations in weather patterns are becoming very common these days, it still feels strange to me to live through them! As I meditate with this remarkable phenomenon, three thoughts come to me, which lead me to a perfect conclusion for this book:

1. According to *Yijing* prediction principles, regular unseasonal weather patterns indicate a world in turmoil. Under these conditions, many things may disturb our experience of daily life. It is important for each of us to find our inner balance in turbulent times, not only to help us maintain our own health and sense of peace, but also to contribute some harmonious energy for the greater benefit of the world at large. I hope the Tiger Qigong form will help you find your inner balance.

2. An incredible amount of grass and vegetation died due to the lack of rain here this summer, which reminds me how vital it is that we place special emphasis on boosting Jing 精, the source of Water in the body. A deficiency of Jing in our body is just as damaging as is a shortage of water in nature, and can set up unfavorable conditions regarding our health and our longevity. Daily Tiger Qigong practice is like creating your own Heavenly Rain, replenishing your Jing every day. I hope you will enjoy the practice.

3. In Daoist tradition, autumn represents the declining age of retirement, while summer symbolizes the strong life energy of an adult at the peak of their life. However, the patterns in nature this autumn and summer remind me that life is not measured chronologically by age. Daoist internal cultivation principles teach us that we can FanLaoHuanTong 返老還童, reverse your

age and return to your young state, if you are able to rebuild your YuanJing 元精, your life source. This Tiger Qigong form is an essential tool to help your discover your Xü 虛 (your inner Tiger's den and life force) and use it to rejuvenate your YuanJing.

Balancing Tiger Qi,

Master Zhongxian Wu

WuXu ChuShu 戊戌處暑 (the midpoint of the first month of Autumn in the Earth Dog Year)

"Phoenix Nest," Sweden